Table of Contents

Title Page

Copyright

Front Matter

Table of Contents

Introduction

The Digital Dilemma

Navigating the Noise

Seeking Serenity in Screens

Understanding Mindfulness

Roots of Mindful Living

Benefits of Being Present

The Mindful Online Presence

Cultivating Awareness in Digital Interactions

Conscious Social Media Use

Digital Detox

Creating Space for Silence

Strategies for Regular Disconnect

Mindful Communication

Engaging with Intent

The Role of Active Listening

The Art of Digital Minimalism

Simplifying Your Digital World

Prioritizing Essential Technologies

Mindful Tech Tools

Apps for Awareness

Gadgets That Promote Clarity

Balancing Work and Digital Rest

Setting Boundaries in a Remote World

Techniques for Digital Down Time

Enhancing Focus in a Distracted World

Techniques for Sustained Attention

Reducing Digital Clutter

The Intersection of Mindfulness and AI

Understanding AI's Impact on Attention

Mindful Integration of AI Tools

Emotional Regulation Online

Managing Digital Stress

Techniques for Handling Online Conflicts

The Role of Digital Mindfulness in Relationships

Nurturing Connections Through Technology

Avoiding the Pitfalls of Digital Miscommunication

Digital Mindfulness for Families

Creating a Balanced Home Environment

Strategies for Mindful Media Consumption

Cultivating Creativity with Mindfulness

Finding Inspiration Online

Mindful Consumption of Creative Content

Mindful Data Consumption

Navigating News with Awareness

Evaluating Digital Information Critically

Harnessing Virtual Reality for Inner Peace

Applications of VR for Meditation

The Future of VR Mindfulness Practices

The Workplace Zen

Mindful Practices for Professional Success

Balancing Productivity with Wellbeing

Mindful Digital Learning

Embracing Education Platforms

Strategies for Focused Online Learning

Guiding Youth Towards Digital Mindfulness

Teaching Children to Navigate Technology

Developing Healthy Digital Habits

Mindful Gaming

Approaching Video Games with Awareness

Positive Gaming Practices

Incorporating Mindful Breaks in Digital Routines

Designing Breaks for Mental Clarity

Practices for Quick Resets

Environmental Impact of Technology

Understanding Digital Footprint

Mindful Consumption of Technology

Privacy and Digital Peace

Protecting Personal Information

Staying Safe and Mindful Online

Mindful Leadership in the Digital Age

Developing Conscious Leadership Qualities

Techniques for Leading with Presence

The Future of Digital Mindfulness

Emerging Trends and Insights

Preparing for Continuous Connection

Conclusion

Appendix

Resources for Further Reading

Digital Zen

Mindfulness in a Hyper-Connected World

by

David Holman

Contents

Introduction

Chapter 1: The Digital Dilemma

Navigating the Noise

Seeking Serenity in Screens

Chapter 2: Understanding Mindfulness

Roots of Mindful Living

Benefits of Being Present

Chapter 3: The Mindful Online Presence

Cultivating Awareness in Digital Interactions

Conscious Social Media Use

Chapter 4: Digital Detox

Creating Space for Silence

Strategies for Regular Disconnect

Chapter 5: Mindful Communication

Engaging with Intent

The Role of Active Listening

Chapter 6: The Art of Digital Minimalism

Simplifying Your Digital World

Prioritizing Essential Technologies

Chapter 7: Mindful Tech Tools

Apps for Awareness

Gadgets That Promote Clarity

Chapter 8: Balancing Work and Digital Rest

Setting Boundaries in a Remote World

Techniques for Digital Down Time

Chapter 9: Enhancing Focus in a Distracted World

Techniques for Sustained Attention

Reducing Digital Clutter

Chapter 10: The Intersection of Mindfulness and AI

Understanding AI's Impact on Attention

Mindful Integration of AI Tools

Chapter 11: Emotional Regulation Online

Managing Digital Stress

Techniques for Handling Online Conflicts

Chapter 12: The Role of Digital Mindfulness in Relationships

Nurturing Connections Through Technology

Avoiding the Pitfalls of Digital Miscommunication

Chapter 13: Digital Mindfulness for Families

Creating a Balanced Home Environment

Strategies for Mindful Media Consumption

Chapter 14: Cultivating Creativity with Mindfulness

Finding Inspiration Online

Mindful Consumption of Creative Content

Chapter 15: Mindful Data Consumption

Navigating News with Awareness

Evaluating Digital Information Critically

Chapter 16: Harnessing Virtual Reality for Inner Peace

Applications of VR for Meditation

The Future of VR Mindfulness Practices

Chapter 17: The Workplace Zen

Mindful Practices for Professional Success

Balancing Productivity with Wellbeing

Chapter 18: Mindful Digital Learning

Embracing Education Platforms

Strategies for Focused Online Learning

Chapter 19: Guiding Youth Towards Digital Mindfulness

Teaching Children to Navigate Technology

Developing Healthy Digital Habits

Chapter 20: Mindful Gaming

Approaching Video Games with Awareness

Positive Gaming Practices

Chapter 21: Incorporating Mindful Breaks in Digital Routines

Designing Breaks for Mental Clarity

Practices for Quick Resets

Chapter 22: Environmental Impact of Technology

Understanding Digital Footprint

Mindful Consumption of Technology

Chapter 23: Privacy and Digital Peace

Protecting Personal Information

Staying Safe and Mindful Online

Chapter 24: Mindful Leadership in the Digital Age

Developing Conscious Leadership Qualities

Techniques for Leading with Presence

Chapter 25: The Future of Digital Mindfulness

Emerging Trends and Insights

Preparing for Continuous Connection

Conclusion

Appendix A: Appendix

Resources for Further Reading

Introduction

In today's world, technology is woven into the fabric of our daily lives. It's everywhere—from the smartphones in our pockets to the tablets on our desks, the apps that manage our to-do lists to the social media platforms that connect us with friends and family across the globe. While this digital connectivity offers unparalleled convenience and communication, it brings with it a deluge of information and a bombardment of notifications, all clamoring for our attention. It's as if our devices have become another appendage, an extension of ourselves that we can't quite detach from.

As a result, many find themselves caught in a paradox. The technologies designed to make life simpler and more connected often end up overwhelming our senses, leaving us stressed, scattered, and constantly tethered to screens. The need to be always available, always updated, and always engaged has created an environment where silence and solitude are luxuries rather than norms. The question then arises: how do we navigate this digital storm while remaining grounded and present in our own lives?

Mindfulness offers a compelling antidote. Rooted in ancient practices and yet more relevant than ever, mindfulness calls for a deep awareness and presence in the current moment. By applying mindful techniques to our interactions with technology, we can begin to cultivate a more harmonious relationship with our digital tools. Instead of being controlled by constant connectivity, we can learn to engage with intention, to find serenity amidst the noise, and to balance digital demands with personal well-being.

This book is a guide for tech-savvy individuals seeking this balance. It highlights the integration of mindful practices into our digital lives, helping you uncover pathways to tranquility through a series of carefully considered approaches. Each chapter explores different facets of digital mindfulness, from understanding the roots and benefits of presence to strategies for detoxing from the digital realm and creating mindful online interactions.

The goal is not to reject technology but to reshape how we experience it. In doing so, we harness its benefits while mitigating its distractions. This mindful approach involves more than just time away from screens; it's also about intentional engagement, being conscious of how we use these tools to enhance rather than diminish our life experiences. By consciously choosing how we engage digitally, we can foster a healthier relationship with technology—one that sustains our mental, emotional, and even physical well-being.

As we delve into the essence of digital mindfulness, you'll discover strategies for managing digital stress, creating mindful communication, and employing technology to inspire rather than inundate. The book also explores the intersection of modern innovations like artificial intelligence and virtual reality with mindful practices, emphasizing not only what we gain from these technologies but also what we may inadvertently lose unless we engage mindfully.

Mindful digital habits extend beyond individual practices; they shape our interactions within relationships, families, and even workplaces. By integrating mindfulness into these facets, we create environments that are not just productive but also nurturing and supportive, where meaningful connections flourish despite the digital medium. It's about steering technology's impact from distraction to empowerment across all areas of life.

This introduction, therefore, sets the stage for a journey into mindfulness in a wired world. Each subsequent chapter builds upon this foundation, crafting a roadmap that guides you towards a more mindful existence in the face of relentless digital demands. It's an invitation to pause, reflect, and engage with technology with a renewed sense of purpose and clarity.

So, embark on this journey towards digital mindfulness. Whether you're looking to declutter your digital life, find serenity amid constant pings and alerts, or integrate mindfulness into everyday interactions, this book offers insight and inspiration. It seeks to empower you to make conscious choices, so you can ultimately reclaim balance and tranquility in a digitally driven world, fostering a life that is not only technologically connected but also deeply and mindfully present.

Chapter 1: The Digital Dilemma

In today's hyper-connected world, the digital dilemma ambushes us at every turn. We navigate through an incessant stream of notifications and emails, our senses overwhelmed by the noise, yet we yearn for moments of peace that seem just out of reach. This relentless connectivity threatens to fracture our inner harmony, leaving us adrift in a sea of screens. But within this storm lies an opportunity—a chance to redefine our relationship with technology, harmonizing the digital and mindful spheres. It's about crafting a life where digital interactions complement rather than control us, transforming the chaos into calm and turning distraction into focused serenity. By embracing mindful practices, we can reclaim our attention, fortifying our spirit against the onslaught of digital demands. Together, let's embark on this journey to rediscover tranquility amidst the turbulence, helping us cultivate a balanced existence in both our screens and our souls.

Navigating the Noise

In today's hyper-connected world, the constant barrage of notifications, alerts, and updates screams for our attention. It can feel like being in a crowded room where everyone's talking at once, and you're expected to listen and respond to every single voice. This overwhelming stimulus, aptly described as digital noise, is a lens through which many perceive the digital world. The challenge is to not only survive but thrive amidst this clamor, finding moments of silence and clarity that help anchor our mental well-being.

The first step in navigating digital noise involves understanding its sources. It's not just the pings from social media; it includes emails, news alerts, advertisements, and even the subtle pressures of staying connected and responsive. Each source, while sometimes valuable, can also act as a potential stressor and distraction. Recognizing what constitutes noise in your digital ecosystem is essential to managing its influence over your time and attention.

To truly chart a path through this noise, one must develop an acute awareness of its personal impact. This means regularly asking yourself: How does this make me feel? Does this add value or merely occupy space? Reflecting on the emotional and mental toll of constant connectivity offers clarity. It's about discerning not just what you engage with, but how it aligns with your values and well-being.

The art of filtering is crucial for sifting through digital chaos. Think of your digital presence like a garden—it requires regular pruning to thrive. This doesn't mean eliminating all digital interaction, but selectively choosing where to focus your energies. Prioritize interactions that enrich your life, nurturing connections and content that inspire growth while weeding out what is purely noise.

Implementing boundaries is a tactical way to reduce digital interference. Simple choices can have profound impacts: scheduling "do not disturb" times, creating tech-free zones in your home, or setting specific times to check emails. These practices aren't about denying the digital world access, but about creating controlled environments in which you can enjoy your digital life without it dictating your day's rhythm.

Mindfulness plays a pivotal role in cultivating this discipline. By centering your awareness on the present moment, you learn to engage with technology in deliberate ways. Each interaction becomes a mindful choice rather than an automatic response. This mindful approach helps transform potential digital distractions into intentional experiences.

One practical exercise is to start each day without immediately reaching for your phone. Instead, spend a few moments in reflection or meditation, setting intentions for how you wish to use technology throughout the day. This simple shift creates a mindset of control and purpose, positioning digital interactions as tools rather than tyrants.

It's also valuable to explore digital tools designed specifically to aid in managing noise. Apps that track screen time, facilitate focused work sessions, or remind you to take breaks can offer tangible support. Similarly, adjusting notification settings ensures that only the most critical information reaches you, providing an essential buffer from unnecessary disruptions.

As you hone these skills, the digital noise begins to fade into the background. You're still aware of its presence, but it no longer consumes your thoughts or dictates your actions. With time, your relationship with technology transforms into one of balance and mutual benefit—not dominance and dependency.

Engaging with technology in mindful ways requires continuous practice and adaptation. The digital landscape constantly evolves, and so must your strategies to navigate it. Stay open to changing routines and trying new approaches as you seek harmony within this ever-changing environment.

Tuning into your inner needs above external demands ensures a more peaceful balance amid life's hustle and bustle. By prioritizing this equilibrium, the noise becomes manageable, and your digital world turns into a space of creativity, connectivity, and calm.

Seeking Serenity in Screens

In the cacophony of our digital lives, finding moments of true tranquility can feel like searching for a needle in a virtual haystack. The very screens that inundate us with information have the potential to become tools for serenity. But how do we shift our mindset to repurpose these screens for moments of peace rather than perpetual distraction?

Consider the smartphone—a device often accused of fragmenting our attention. Yet, it's also a gateway to guided meditations, calming soundscapes, and digital minimalism apps designed to reduce screen time. It's ironic, perhaps, that the solution to our tech-induced stress lies, in part, in the technology itself. What if we could transform our relationship with our screens, turning them into allies in our pursuit of mindfulness rather than adversaries?

A key aspect of this transformation is *intention*. Too often, screen time is passive—a mindless scroll through social media or a binge on streaming services. By approaching our digital interactions with intention, we can shift from passive consumption to active engagement. This means questioning why we're reaching for our devices and considering whether they're serving our present needs. Are we connecting with someone meaningful? Learning something new? Or simply filling a void?

For many, screens are intertwined with their professional lives. The constant emails, notifications, and updates can feel inescapable. However, by consciously choosing windows of time for digital engagement, we can create boundaries that foster peace. Scheduling "tech-free" periods during the day can provide a mental reset, enhancing focus and reducing stress.

Moreover, not all screen interactions are created equal. Engaging in activities that foster creativity, learning, or relaxation can be immensely rewarding. Immersing oneself in a documentary or engaging with a creative app can stimulate the mind in positive ways. It's not about eliminating screen time but curating it to align with our values and goals.

Despite the tempting allure of digital distraction, there's a growing movement toward turning screens into spaces for mindfulness. Platforms offering guided mindfulness practices, live-streaming yoga classes, or even virtual reality environments focused on relaxation show that the potential for digital serenity is vast.

Mindful technology doesn't just benefit individuals—it holds promise for our communities as well. Consider video calls as platforms for genuine connection rather than mundane meetings, providing opportunities to foster deeper relationships, even across distances. The challenge lies in utilizing these opportunities mindfully, ensuring that digital interactions aren't just superficial replacements for face-to-face conversations but meaningful exchanges in their own right.

As we explore the role of mindfulness in our digital lives, it's essential to remember that technology is not the enemy. Screens are not inherently good or bad—they're vessels, shaped by how we choose to engage with them. By embracing this perspective, we can navigate our digital world with greater awareness and intention.

Embodying tranquility in our screen use doesn't mean avoiding technology altogether. It's about harnessing it for personal growth and mental well-being. By prioritizing meaningful digital interactions, limiting exposure to negative content, and being selective about the time we spend on screens, we can create a balance that supports our peace of mind.

Ultimately, the journey towards digital mindfulness requires practice and patience. It's a commitment to self-awareness and adaptability as our digital landscape continues to evolve. By seeking serenity in screens, we're not merely avoiding distraction; we're crafting a digital experience that's both enriching and fulfilling.

Chapter 2: Understanding Mindfulness

In this era of relentless connectivity, understanding mindfulness offers a reprieve, a chance to pause amidst the digital chaos. Mindfulness, at its core, is about cultivating a present-focused awareness, free from distraction and judgment. It invites us to step back, observe our thoughts, and embrace the present with intention and clarity. By weaving mindfulness into our daily routine, we can foster a balance between the digital world and our internal landscape. Mindfulness enables us to consciously engage with technology, rather than being consumed by it, preserving our mental well-being while navigating the flood of digital stimuli. Let mindfulness be your anchor, guiding you to find peace in each moment, even amidst the fervor of our tech-driven lives.

Roots of Mindful Living

Understanding the roots of mindful living offers a gateway not only to tranquility but also to an enriched, intentional life amidst the cacophony of a digitally-driven world. Mindfulness, in its essence, is about presence—being acutely aware of the here and now. Its origins trace back millennia, embedded within ancient traditions that recognized the power of full attention to moment-to-moment experiences. This practice has grown ever more relevant as the digital age challenges our capacity to remain focused and engaged in the present.

At its heart, mindful living is deeply entwined with the teachings of Buddhism but is not confined to a single religious perspective. It invites individuals from all walks of life to slow down, observe their thoughts and feelings without judgment, and engage with reality as it unfolds. The basic tenets encompass being fully engaged in what you're doing, acknowledging the impermanence of thoughts, and cultivating a sense of acceptance over the internal and external events of life. These principles stand in stark contrast to the duty cycle of notifications and perpetual connectivity that defines today's digital humanity.

For the tech-savvy yet overwhelmed individual, mindful living provides a runway to reclaim attention, navigate digital landscapes with intention, and ultimately live more fulfilling lives. Mindfulness empowers us to pause, reflect, and respond instead of reacting instinctively. This is particularly vital given the omnipresent temptation to multitask, with myriad screens vying for our focus. Returning to these roots encourages us to make deliberate choices about where our attention goes, fostering mental clarity and emotional resilience.

These foundational elements of mindfulness stem from a universal need for connection—both inwardly to oneself and outwardly to the world. Ancient practices encourage practitioners to engage with what is real rather than the artificial constructs that digital environments so often present. This isn't to say that technology is detrimental; rather, it's about harmonizing technology use with attentive living. By acknowledging—and addressing—the cognitive discord instigated by constant connectivity, mindfulness offers a methodology for weaving tranquility into one's digital experiences.

Moreover, there's wisdom in understanding that while technology evolves at an alarming pace, our human brains haven't kept up quite the same relentless rate. These ancient practices provide tools to respect the limitations of our mental faculties. By planting our roots in mindful living, we create a psychological space where technology serves us, not overwhelms us. Mindfulness inspires a digital ethos that focuses on quality rather than the quantity of interactions, guiding individuals towards meaningful digital experiences over hollow engagements.

Practicing mindfulness doesn't mean adopting an austere lifestyle devoid of technology; rather, it advocates for balance. It's about nurturing one's ability to be fully present, regardless of whether you're in a meditative state or scrolling through emails. This calls for cultivating awareness of one's emotional states and recognizing how digital interactions impact them. A mindful approach to living and technology use isn't prescriptive but is rather a personal exploration, a journey to understand better what nurtures each individual's peace and productivity.

As our ancient predecessors knew, enduring peace isn't something that exists on the sidelines of life's rollercoaster. Mindful living teaches that it is woven through the warp and weft of daily actions, thoughts, and moments of connectivity. Cultivating such awareness inevitably introduces a sense of gratitude, often absent in digital pursuits where one is perpetually seeking the next big thing. By anchoring oneself in the present and acknowledging here and now, a reservoir of contentment becomes available.

A mindful living foundation probes deeper than surface-level enrichment, engendering a profound appreciation for the simplicity of life unencumbered by external noise. It's about refocusing priorities, valuing experiences over acquisitions, relationships over followers. In doing so, one paves the way for genuine interaction, a rarity in a world of filtered realities. This interaction enriches not only the personal sphere but extends to how we professionally and socially conduct ourselves.

Ultimately, the roots of mindful living invite us to redefine our relationship with technology, encouraging introspection to discern its rightful place within our lives. Whether we're navigating an overcrowded email inbox or curating a social media profile, embodying the principles of mindful living allows us to approach these tasks with a measured sense of calm and clarity. It's a call to action that reminds us that in a world designed to distract, there is tremendous power in consciously choosing where we place our focus.

In this pursuit of a balanced digital existence, the roots of mindful living serve as both a reminder and a call to action, drawing from timeless wisdom to inform our modern lives. They champion a path where intentional presence becomes the counterbalance to the ever-pressing demands of connectivity, enabling individuals to flourish within the digital world without being consumed by it.

Benefits of Being Present

In our fast-paced digital world, the idea of being present might seem almost radical. Yet, this simple practice is increasingly seen as vital for maintaining mental clarity and emotional well-being. At its core, being present means truly embracing the moment you are in, without distractions or mental wanderings. This state of awareness allows you to experience life fully instead of skimming through the surface as our digital habits often encourage us to do.

The benefits of practicing presence extend beyond peace of mind, activating a profound shift in how we interact with both our digital and analog worlds. When we are present, we become more attuned to our surroundings and the people we engage with, allowing us to form deeper connections. In the context of a digital lifestyle, this means that you may start choosing quality over quantity in your communications, prioritizing meaningful interactions over countless, shallow ones.

For the tech-savvy individual, always plugged into devices, the ability to consciously disconnect, even momentarily, provides a sense of freedom. This intentional state of presence negates the constant barrage of notifications and information. It helps mitigate the often overwhelming sense of digital noise that permeates our daily lives. By being present, you build a refuge from the relentless stream of online stimuli, giving your mind space to breathe and your thoughts room to grow beyond the next ping.

Moreover, being present sharpens your focus. Instead of spreading your cognitive resources too thin across multiple tasks, you can concentrate on one task with full attention. This focused attention not only boosts productivity but also enhances the quality of whatever you are working on. You become meticulous in your efforts, excelling in tasks that require creativity, problem-solving, or any form of deep work. It's like trading instant gratification for long-term fulfillment which resonates more deeply.

In terms of emotional health, the presence anchors you in reality, helping you to respond rather than react. This mindful state can significantly enhance your stress management techniques. Being present allows you to observe but not immediately act on, the emotional currents that arise when you encounter challenging online interactions or stressful work emails. This practice builds emotional resilience, increasing your capacity to cope with digital stress and reducing the likelihood of being swept away by emotional surges.

Your social interactions also benefit from your presence. In an age where relationships are often mediated through screens, being fully present when communicating can be transformative. It encourages authentic engagement and reduces misunderstandings— components essential for nurturing any relationship, whether with family, friends, or colleagues. The capacity to genuinely listen and respond can make interactions much more satisfying and fulfilling.

Here's a compelling advantage: presence can sharpen your digital literacy. In a world where misinformation spreads fast and furiously, being present enhances your ability to critically analyze and process the deluge of information you consume. You become a more discerning digital navigator, adept at recognizing credible sources and skeptical of those that aren't. This conscious consumption makes you a less susceptible target for digital manipulation.

The practice of being present can also significantly enhance your creativity. When your mind is not tethered to the past or the future—two states of being that digital platforms often nudge us towards—you have an unparalleled opportunity to engage in creative thinking. A present state of mind is fertile ground for ideas to flourish, free from the constraints of worry about what has been or what might be.

The physiological benefits of presence are just as potent. Mindfulness practices that cultivate presence can lower cortisol levels, which reduces stress and supports immune function. The mere act of being in the moment—whether it's focusing on your breathing, being aware of your surroundings without judgment, or engaging fully with a task—can reduce chronic stress that so often results from living in a persistently connected world.

Despite all these benefits, being present in the digital age poses unique challenges. With constant notifications and digital devices programmed to capture and hold our attention, it requires a conscious effort to harness the power of being present. Yet, no matter how impervious our digital landscapes appear, the human capacity to cultivate awareness is remarkably resilient and adaptable.

Incorporating presence into everyday life doesn't require drastic measures or a complete digital detox. Small habitual changes—like setting boundaries on device usage, allocating specific times for consuming digital content, or practicing mindfulness exercises before engaging with technology—can create a foundation for being present. These intentional practices encourage a balance where technology and mindfulness coexist without one overshadowing the other.

By practicing presence, you can transform your relationship with technology. Instead of seeing your devices as conduits for endless information and constant communication, you can use them as tools to enhance your mindfulness practices in practical ways. Your calendar can become a space for scheduling moments of presence, or a simple app can remind you to take mindful breaks throughout your day.

Presence doesn't mean abandoning the digital world but redefining how you interact with it. This redefinition is a path toward navigating life with mindful intention, enabling you to live with more awareness, more joy, and less stress. As you embrace this practice, the benefits of being present become not just a chapter in the story of your digital life but a cornerstone of a life well-lived.

Chapter 3: The Mindful Online Presence

In the relentless ebb and flow of notifications and updates, creating a mindful online presence is crucial for those seeking peace amidst digital chaos. It's about consciously engaging with screens and digital platforms, not as passive consumers but as intentional participants. Mindfulness in the digital realm means pausing before responding, assessing the value of engagement, and embracing digital interactions with full awareness. By becoming more attuned to how you connect online, you invite a shift—from mindless scrolling to enriching experiences that respect your mental health and time. This chapter offers you an opportunity to cultivate a space where technology enhances, rather than detracts from, your well-being, fostering a sense of serenity no matter how connected you remain. Through mindful practices, you'll learn to balance digital life with presence and purpose, allowing technology to serve you rather than overwhelm you. In doing so, you empower yourself to interact with the digital world in a way that aligns with your values and enhances your life's quality.

Cultivating Awareness in Digital Interactions

In an era where screens dominate our lives, pausing to cultivate awareness in our digital interactions can be transformative. We find ourselves perpetually connected, pinged by the latest notifications, scrolling through endless feeds. Yet, amidst this digital clutter, there's an overlooked opportunity for mindfulness. This awareness isn't about turning away from our devices but engaging with them more thoughtfully. Mindfulness teaches us to be present, to engage authentically, and to recognize the impact of our actions online.

At its core, cultivating awareness in digital interactions begins with intention. How do we feel when we reach for our phone or open a browser? Are we acting out of habit or seeking genuine connection? By questioning these impulses, we create space for conscious choices instead of reflexive actions. This simple act of pausing can shift our entire online experience, anchoring it in presence rather than mindlessness. Next time you're about to engage online, take a breath and ask yourself what you genuinely hope to achieve.

The digital realm offers a unique anonymity that can undermine our interpersonal interactions. Comments become more aggressive, opinions hardened without the softening presence of face-to-face communication. Recognizing the humanity behind the usernames we interact with is essential. Visualization techniques can help us here. Before replying to a post or sending a message, take a moment to visualize the person on the other side—imagine their tone, their expressions. Such awareness can transform our digital engagements from antagonistic exchanges to empathetic conversations.

A significant aspect of digital awareness involves our consumption patterns. How often do we find ourselves lost in an information vortex, jumping from one article to another, barely remembering what initiated the journey? This kind of mindless browsing not only drains time but also mental energy. To counter this, set clear intentions before diving online. Know what you're looking to know or achieve, and remind yourself of it if you start to drift.

Our awareness isn't limited to the content we consume; it extends to how we contribute to the digital world. Sharing and creating should be acts filled with intention. When posting an article, a thought, or even a photograph, it's worth considering its purpose. What's my intention behind this post? How might it affect others? By instilling intention in our contributions, we not only enhance our own experience but also uplift the communal digital space.

Interruptions are another arena where digital mindfulness plays a critical role. The constant buzz of notifications can scatter our focus and diminish our productivity. By understanding and reclaiming control over these interruptions, we promote a healthier relationship with technology. A simple step is to evaluate which notifications are necessary and which add to the noise. Prioritize what truly matters and let go of the rest. This small adjustment alone can bring about a profound sense of clarity.

Moreover, digital spaces present opportunities for deepened self-awareness. As we interact online, we can observe our emotions and reactions: What brings joy? What triggers stress? Mindfulness encourages an exploration of these patterns. Journaling after spending time online can be beneficial. Capture thoughts and feelings that emerged, identifying those triggers and joys. Over time, patterns will emerge, guiding more mindful digital engagement.

Digital interactions, too, call for a sense of pause and reflection. Just as in traditional communication, the spaces between actions can speak volumes. Before jumping to respond to an email or message, consider employing a pause. This delay fosters a calmer, more considered response and diminishes the potential for misunderstanding.

The path to digital mindfulness is neither linear nor one-size-fits-all. It's a personal journey of trial and reflection, adapting practices that resonate most. Some might find solace in scheduled digital detoxes or in setting specific times for screen use. Others may explore switching digital devices for analog alternatives when engaging in particular activities, like reading. The key is experimenting with ways that best nurture one's digital and mental clarity.

Finally, awareness in digital interactions expands into the realm of gratitude. Amongst the noise, there's much for which to be thankful. Technology connects us with loved ones across miles, delivers knowledge to our fingertips, and empowers social movements. By cultivating gratitude for these benefits, we can shift our relationship with technology from a source of overwhelm to one of appreciation. A gratitude practice could involve noting down three positive digital interactions each day, fostering a mindset of thankfulness.

The journey toward a mindful online presence is continuous. It's about acknowledging the present moment in each swipe, scroll, and click. With practice, we balance the digital world's demands while maintaining our peace of mind, moving from reactive use to intentional engagement. With each interaction, consider: How can I bring more mindfulness to this moment? In doing so, we transform not just our digital engagements but our consciousness, paving the way for a more harmonious relationship with technology.

Conscious Social Media Use

Social media, for many of us, acts like a magnet pulling us into its orbit, capturing our attention with its endless scroll. Its power to connect is undeniable, yet the way it immerses us often feels more consuming than enriching. Cultivating a conscious approach to social media can be liberating, allowing us to reclaim attention while fostering meaningful connections and self-awareness. The key lies in shifting our mindset from mindless consumption to intentional engagement.

Imagine opening an app and engaging purposefully rather than reflexively. This practice requires noticing our motivations for logging on: Are we seeking validation, distraction, or genuine connection? By becoming aware of the "why" behind our social media use, we can pivot toward activities that fulfill our true needs rather than superficial ones. Such introspection can unveil patterns of use that may not align with our values or well-being.

Reflect on the content you encounter—what emotional responses do they evoke, and how do they impact your self-esteem and worldview? Curating your feed with a discerning eye can turn social media into a tool for inspiration rather than a source of anxiety. Unfollow accounts that lead to comparison or negativity, and instead choose to engage with those that provide value and positivity.

Taking control of notifications is another small change with significant impact. Notifications are designed to snatch our attention at any moment, interrupting tasks and thoughts. By turning off non-essential alerts, or scheduling specific times to check for updates, we become less reactive and more present with ourselves and others around us. This deliberate action fosters a healthier relationship with technology.

Set boundaries around your social media usage. Designate tech-free zones or times in your routine—for example, during meals or before bed. These boundaries encourage you to engage with the physical world and the people within it, providing much-needed mental space to reflect and recharge. Something as simple as leaving your phone in another room can enforce breaks from digital noise.

Practicing compassion and empathy online is as important as the conversations we have in person. Before posting or commenting, pause to consider if your words contribute positively to the dialogue. Personal interactions, even in digital spaces, shape our experience and the experiences of others. Take the time to engage in meaningful conversations and offer support when possible.

Mindfulness in social media also involves understanding its algorithm-driven nature. Algorithms are built to serve us content that will hold our gaze, often at the expense of diversity and critical engagement. By actively seeking varied perspectives and questioning the mono-directional flow of information, we inject intention into our online presence.

Engage with content that challenges your views and enriches your understanding of the world.

Taking social media breaks is another vital component of conscious use. Stepping away from the screen can be refreshing, helping us to disconnect from the barrage of information and reconnect with our inner selves. This conscious disconnection doesn't mean renouncing social media altogether; rather, it is about creating space for presence and clarity amidst digital overwhelm.

If you choose to document your life online, do it mindfully. When capturing moments, ask yourself if the impulse to share is enhancing the experience or detracting from it. Authenticity online can become a practice of mindfulness itself. Acknowledge if the act of sharing pulls you away from the joy of the present or if it adds meaning to your interactions with the global community.

Ultimately, turning social media into a mindful practice involves infusing it with the same awareness we aim to bring into our offline lives. It's about cultivating a sense of presence and self-awareness amidst the digital landscape, creating space for ourselves where technology often doesn't. By transforming how we interact online, we discover an avenue for balanced, rewarding social engagement.

Chapter 4: Digital Detox

In an era where constant digital noise seems inevitable, embarking on a digital detox offers a sanctuary for the overwhelmed mind. Just as our bodies benefit from fasting, so too do our minds find clarity when we disconnect from the relentless streams of information. This temporary escape allows you to create space for silence, cultivating moments of profound stillness in a hyper-connected world. It's a chance to reclaim your attention by setting boundaries, perhaps by designating tech-free zones or specific times for unplugging, encouraging a mindful dialogue with the technology that surrounds us. Through consistent practice, this intentional disconnect becomes a revitalizing habit, serving as a powerful reminder that your digital life is a choice, not a compulsion. Engaging in such detoxes doesn't mean forsaking the digital world; instead, it means embracing it with renewed presence and purpose.

Creating Space for Silence

In our hyperconnected age, silence has become a rare commodity, often undervalued and overlooked. It's easy to fill every moment with noise, from the incessant pinging of notifications to the endless scroll of social media. Yet, it's within silence that we truly discover ourselves and the present moment. Carving out intentional blocks of quietude allows us to step back, breathe, and recalibrate our minds amidst the digital cacophony.

Cultivating silence isn't just about escaping noise; it's about creating an environment where thoughts can unfold naturally. In silence, we invite mindfulness to seep into our consciousness. It provides a canvas where ideas can emerge without disruption, where internal dialogues don't fight for attention in a sea of external stimuli. When we purposefully create these spaces, we foster introspection and contemplation, two components often drowned out by constant connectivity.

But how do we begin? Start small. Designate specific moments throughout your day dedicated to silence. Perhaps it's during your morning coffee or your evening routine. Turn off your devices, even if just for ten minutes. Close your eyes, focus on your breath, and listen intently to the world around you. In those moments, clarity starts to surface, and you begin to reconnect with a part of yourself long overshadowed by the digital realm.

Maintaining a sanctuary of silence amid bustling digital environments is a practice of detachment. This doesn't mean rejecting technology altogether; rather, it's about learning when to step back. Just like a gardener prunes a plant to encourage growth, pruning noise from your life creates room for mindfulness to flourish. It allows you to approach technology consciously, appreciating its benefits without surrendering your peace.

The process of creating silence also transforms our interactions with digital devices. We learn to use technology purposefully, rather than passively engaging with whatever appears on our screens. Silence offers us the power to pause and reflect, enabling us to determine what truly deserves our attention. It encourages thoughtful consumption, nudging us to question what adds value versus what clutters our minds.

Incorporating silence into a daily routine requires a gentle shift in perception. See it not as an absence of sound, but as a presence of tranquility. Embrace it as a powerful practice that nurtures the soul. Recognize the transformative potential of silence to heal and ground you in a world that's constantly in motion. This mindful reorientation towards silence can bring profound insights and renewed energy.

Silence isn't solely about individual enrichment; it resonates through our relationships as well. By practicing silence, we enhance our capacity to listen and connect more deeply with others. It allows us to offer our full, undivided attention when needed. Conversations become richer, empathy swells, and mutual understanding blossoms—qualities easily suppressed by digital distractions.

Given today's pace of life, it might seem counterintuitive to slow down deliberately. Yet, the impact of silence reverberates through every aspect of our well-being. Just as an artist steps back to perceive the whole canvas, so does silence grant us a broader view of our lives. It's from this vantage point that strategic decisions emerge, helping us navigate not just the digital world but the complexities of being human.

Ultimately, creating space for silence is a commitment to preserve what's sacred within us. It's a pledge to honor our need for reflection and grounding in a digital world that rarely pauses. This practice doesn't demand grand gestures. It's found in the simple act of being still, in the quiet moments that bookend our day, and in the conscious choice to listen within.

Embrace the stillness, for within it lies a path to peace. Silence, when cultivated with intent, becomes a powerful ally in our journey toward digital harmony and mindful living. Allow it to guide you, to enrich your connection with the world and yourself, anchoring you firmly in the present moment where true tranquility resides.

Strategies for Regular Disconnect

Finding a regular rhythm for disconnecting in our hyper-connected world is not just a luxury; it's a necessity. The digital age brings with it a barrage of notifications, emails, and social media updates that can hijack our attention and cloud our mindfulness. Establishing a mindful routine for regular disconnect helps us reclaim our focus and align our digital habits with intentional living. This section explores practical strategies to ensure that disconnecting becomes an enriching part of our daily lives rather than a sporadic need.

Firstly, set clear intentions about your need for disconnection. Consider why you want to incorporate regular periods away from digital devices. It could be for mental clarity, deeper personal connections, or simply to recharge. When the intention is clear, it becomes much easier to prioritize and rationalize those moments of disconnect. Begin by examining your current relationships with your devices and online platforms. Are they serving you, or simply overwhelming you? Understanding this distinction helps in crafting a more deliberate approach to digital interactions.

An effective strategy is scheduling dedicated "no-tech" times. These can be as short as 15 minutes a day or as long as a full digital sabbatical during weekends. Consistency is key. For example, consider instituting a tech-free hour after dinner every night, turning it into a cherished time for reflection, reading, or family conversations. Scheduling regular digital detox moments acts as a disciplined practice that guards against tech-induced anxiety and fosters mindfulness.

Moreover, create sacred spaces free from technology. Designate certain areas in your home, such as your dining room or bedroom, as gadget-free zones. Not only does this enhance focus, but it also instills a deeper sense of peace and intention. When certain spaces are reserved for connection with oneself or loved ones, it diminishes the pull of the digital world. We start associating these spaces with offline experiences and authentic interactions, reinforcing their importance in our lives.

Equally important is learning to manage notifications smartly. Our devices are preconfigured to grab attention at every opportunity, but subtle changes to settings can make a big difference. Turn off non-essential notifications or employ settings like "Do Not Disturb" during specific times of your day. Taking control of your digital interruptions allows you to maintain attention on what truly matters in any given moment.

Take advantage of technology's settings for self-regulation. Most devices and applications now feature built-in tools to monitor screen time or pause notifications. Use these features to gain insights into your habits and adjust them as necessary. By setting screen time limits or scheduling downtime, you become consciously aware of your digital consumption patterns and can proactively make changes towards a more balanced life.

Another approach is embracing mindfulness practices during everyday activities. While cooking, walking, or commuting, deliberately choose not to engage with your gadgets unless it's necessary. Immerse yourself fully in the task at hand, appreciating every detail, every sensation. Redirecting your attention to the physical world enhances presence and diminishes stress, fostering an authentic disconnection from the digital realm.

Establish routines that bolster a healthy tech-life balance. Find joy in non-digital hobbies that can serve as a natural disconnect. It could be gardening, painting, or playing a musical instrument. These activities not only provide a reprieve from the screen but also allow you to express creativity and gain a sense of accomplishment.

Incorporating mindful breathing exercises or meditation sessions right before and after work can transform how you interact with digital devices. This creates a mental buffer between your personal and digital worlds, reducing stress and enhancing your focus throughout the day. Commit to just five minutes of deep breathing or meditation to center yourself and set the tone for mindful digital engagement.

Social accountability is another powerful tool for regular disconnect. Share your digital detox goals with friends, family, or even online communities. Having a supportive network keeps motivation high while fostering shared experiences. You might find others inspired to join you on your journey to digital mindfulness, creating opportunities for collective growth and connection.

Consider the concept of "digital Sabbaths" – a full day each week entirely free from digital devices. While it may seem daunting, committing to a digital Sabbath can recalibrate your week, offering a profound sense of relaxation and renewal. Use this day to engage in activities that nourish your mind and spirit, reinforcing the gains from your digital detox.

Regularly disconnecting in such a digitally demanding era is a continuous journey rather than a destination. It requires consistent reflection and adjustment. Stay attuned to how these strategies impact your level of connectedness and peace. Let digital mindfulness become an ongoing practice that evolves with you, always remaining in tune with your changing needs and circumstances.

Ultimately, remember that strategies for regular disconnect go beyond merely turning off devices. They're about aligning your digital interactions with mindfulness and intentional living. As you navigate this balance, you'll find that regular disconnection invites a new form of clarity and presence into everyday life. Embrace it as a transformative practice that enriches your journey toward a more mindful existence.

Chapter 5: Mindful Communication

In an age where messages ping faster than thoughts and conversations drift into distractions, mindful communication stands as a beacon of clarity and connection. It's about weaving intent into every word we exchange—whether face-to-face or through the digital ether. This chapter invites you to explore the art of engaging with purpose and presence, allowing conversations to be not just heard but truly understood. By integrating active listening into our repertoire, we transform mundane interactions into meaningful dialogues, fostering empathy and connection. As we navigate this digital age, cultivating mindful communication is not just a choice but a necessity, helping us reclaim tranquility and depth in our connectivity without the constant pull of distractions.

Engaging with Intent

In a world where conversations can occur with a quick click or an instant tap, the art of communication is transforming rapidly. The surge of digital interaction offers endless opportunities yet presents unique challenges. The question becomes: how do we ensure our communications remain meaningful and genuine? Engaging with intent, especially in the digital realm, requires a conscious commitment to crafting exchanges that resonate deeply and authentically.

Intentional engagement, at its core, involves a deliberate approach to communication. It's about focusing on the quality of interactions rather than the quantity. When we're bombarded with notifications, messages, and virtual meetings, there's a temptation to skim through conversations, reacting quickly and sometimes thoughtlessly. But how often do we pause to consider the impact of our words or the emotions we convey through digital platforms?

To engage with intent, we first have to slow down. This might seem counterintuitive in fast-paced digital dialogues, but slowing down creates space for mindfulness. By taking a moment to breathe, consider our thoughts, and connect with our emotions, we can craft messages that are not only clear and concise but also compassionate and considerate. This pause is the foundation of mindful communication.

Words hold immense power. They can uplift, inform, hurt, or heal. In digital communications, the absence of physical cues, like tone of voice or body language, makes our choice of words even more crucial. Every emoji, punctuation mark, and carefully chosen phrase contributes to the message's overall impact. Writing with thoughtfulness and care can transform a mundane interaction into a meaningful exchange.

Listening plays a pivotal role in engaging with intent. While this might seem more relevant in face-to-face conversations, active listening is crucial in digital dialogues too. It means truly focusing on the other person's message rather than merely waiting for our turn to respond. Whether we're reading an email, a text, or a social media comment, attentive reading allows us to understand deeper meanings and respond thoughtfully, rather than react reflexively.

One effective strategy is to employ reflective responses. In practice, this involves paraphrasing or summarizing the other person's message before sharing your thoughts. This not only confirms you've understood them correctly but also shows the speaker that you're genuinely engaged. Such practices foster deeper connections and mutual respect, key components of mindful communication.

Setting clear intentions before engaging in digital communication can also elevate the quality of exchanges. Ask yourself: What is my goal with this interaction? Do I aim to inform, support, or learn? By being clear with our purpose, our communications become more aligned with our values, ensuring our digital presence is both purposeful and impactful.

Moreover, it's essential to reassess the platforms we use for communication. Digital tools should not only facilitate connection but also complement our intention to communicate mindfully. Choosing the right channel for the right message is crucial. For instance, delicate matters might be better suited for a video call or a voice note rather than a text message, where nuances can be easily overlooked.

Another aspect to consider is practicing gratitude in our communications. Expressing genuine appreciation can transform the dynamic of any exchange. Whether it's thanking a colleague for their support or acknowledging a friend's time, gratitude enhances connection and creates a positive feedback loop, encouraging more mindful interactions in the future.

Mindful communication isn't just about the words we use; it's about cultivating presence. This means being fully engaged in the moment, undistracted by other digital stimuli. When composing a message or responding to a communication, it's valuable to give it your undivided attention. Multitasking can dilute the quality of our interactions, leading to misunderstandings or missed opportunities for connection.

Social media platforms, with their rapid-fire exchanges and constant updates, can make engaging with intent particularly challenging. Yet, they also present a unique opportunity to practice and hone mindful communication skills. By setting boundaries, such as allocating specific times for checking notifications or engaging in conversations, we can create a balanced environment that fosters intentional interactions.

Ultimately, engaging with intent isn't a one-time effort but a continuous practice. It involves regularly reflecting on our communication habits, assessing what works, and what doesn't, and making adjustments accordingly. Embracing mindfulness in our interactions can lead to more fulfilling connections, reduced digital stress, and a greater sense of contentment in our digital lives.

As we navigate the complexities of modern communication, it's crucial to remember that every interaction offers an opportunity to connect meaningfully. By approaching conversations, whether online or offline, with intentionality and care, we not only improve the quality of our communications but also enrich our relationships and enhance our personal well-being.

In the journey to harmonize our digital lives with mindful practices, engaging with intent stands as a cornerstone. Through deliberate and thoughtful communication, we cultivate deeper connections, foster understanding, and contribute to a more compassionate and mindful digital world.

The Role of Active Listening

In our bustling digital world, where notifications ping incessantly and screens vie for our attention, the art of active listening can seem a relic of a bygone era. Yet, embracing this skill is a transformative step toward achieving mindful communication. It's an antidote to the pervasive noise, a means to genuinely connect with ourselves and others amidst the chaos of connectivity. By honing our ability to actively listen, we can foster interactions that are not only more meaningful but also more nourishing for the soul.

Active listening is a practice that demands attention. It requires us to set aside distractions, both physical and digital, and focus entirely on the person speaking. This isn't just about hearing words; it's about comprehending feelings and intentions behind those words. In an era where multitasking is often seen as a badge of honor, actively listening asks us to do the opposite: to single-task, to be totally present in a conversation. This is where mindfulness intersects with communication.

Imagine a conversation where each participant feels truly heard and understood. This transformative experience holds the potential to create deeper bonds and foster mutual respect. Active listening enhances these possibilities by encouraging us to engage with intent. Instead of thinking about what to say next, we focus on absorbing the speaker's message. This shift in approach not only enriches our personal conversations but also amplifies professional interactions, making teamwork more collaborative and innovative.

One crucial aspect of active listening is the practice of being fully present. In a world filled with potential distractions, this can be challenging. Notifications, emails, and the allure of other screens can pull us away from the here and now. The choice to put away our devices signifies respect for the speaker and the dialogue. It shows that we value the relationship enough to be mentally and emotionally invested. This investment is a building block for trust, a fundamental aspect of any meaningful relationship.

Practicing active listening also involves acknowledging the speaker's perspective. It's about approaching conversations with empathy, which is a cornerstone of mindful communication. We don't just listen to respond; we listen to understand. This empathetic stance allows us to see beyond our biases and expectations, opening the door to genuine connections—connections that are not just transactional but transformative in nature.

Silence plays a significant role in active listening. While it may seem counterintuitive, silence is a powerful communication tool. It gives speakers the space they need to express their thoughts fully and encourages them to delve deeper into their feelings. Our silence signifies our attentiveness, sending a strong message of respect and interest. This doesn't mean we disengage; rather, we are fully alert, processing what we hear, allowing our responses to be thoughtful and considerate.

Feedback is another vital element of active listening. It requires us to reflect back what we've heard, asking clarifying questions when necessary. These simple acts demonstrate that we are engaged and care about understanding the message accurately. Feedback not only reassures the speaker but also helps to dispel any misunderstandings before they escalate, fostering a more open and honest communication environment.

Incorporating active listening into digital interactions is equally crucial. Online communication often strips away the non-verbal cues that enrich face-to-face conversations. Here, active listening involves reading between the lines and being attuned to tone, punctuation, and context. Whether it's a video call or an email thread, striving to be present and attentive can make a vast difference in how messages are received and understood.

Moreover, digital exchanges benefit greatly from pausing before responding. This pause— an online equivalent of silence—allows us to absorb information fully and craft responses that are thoughtful rather than impulsive. It's a moment of reflection that mirrors a core tenet of mindfulness: responding with intention rather than reacting out of habit. This thoughtful engagement can prevent misunderstandings and promote clearer, more effective communication.

Active listening also cultivates a mindset of continuous learning. Every conversation is an opportunity to discover new perspectives and insights. By actively seeking out and valuing diverse viewpoints, we enrich our understanding and nurture our capacity for empathy. This habit is vital in our interconnected world where diversity is the norm rather than the exception. Active listening encourages us to approach each interaction as a learning opportunity, an avenue for growth and enlightenment.

For those who feel overwhelmed by constant connectivity, active listening offers a pathway to tranquility. It shifts our focus away from the scattered noise of the digital world and redirects it towards meaningful human connections. By fostering deeper, more genuine interactions, active listening helps us see through the superficiality of digital exchanges, reminding us of the value of slowing down and truly engaging with one another.

Ultimately, the role of active listening in mindful communication cannot be overstated. It transforms the way we engage, shifting interactions from being mere exchanges of information to being profound encounters that resonate with understanding and empathy. In a fast-paced, digitally dominated world, the act of truly listening—to others and ourselves—becomes a powerful act of mindfulness. Embraced wholeheartedly, active listening opens avenues for richer relationships and a more harmonious existence within the digital landscape.

Chapter 6: The Art of Digital Minimalism

In the midst of our buzzing digital lives, adopting digital minimalism can be a breath of fresh air. Think of it as more than just a tidy desktop; it's a philosophy that encourages you to carefully discern between what's necessary and what's superfluous. By focusing on essential technologies that truly enhance your life, you create digital spaces that don't overwhelm but instead support your mindful journey. Imagine that your digital world reflects a serene clarity, where apps and gadgets don't dictate your time but enrich it. This approach not only helps you find balance but also fosters a sense of peace, making space for more mindful moments. Let go of the digital chaos, and your everyday experiences might just transform into a dance of simplicity and profound presence.

Simplifying Your Digital World

In the hustle and bustle of our always-on digital age, the clutter of apps, notifications, and devices can become overwhelming. Everyone's felt the pressure that comes from juggling too many digital commitments, and that's why it's essential to step back and assess what's truly necessary. Simplifying your digital world isn't about discarding technology altogether but thoughtfully curating what genuinely adds value to your life.

Start by identifying the core technologies that play pivotal roles in your daily routines. These are the applications and services that not only streamline your tasks but also bring a degree of joy or productivity. Strip away everything else—those redundant apps gathering digital dust on your phone or those endless browser tabs you promised to read later. It might feel like a loss initially, but there's a unique freedom in letting go of the non-essential.

Consider creating a hierarchy for your digital tools. An *essential* tool is indispensable; perhaps it's the email app that keeps you connected to important communications or a calendar that prevents you from missing critical appointments. Next, categorize those tools which enhance your productivity or well-being but aren't critical. Finally, those casual distractions or redundant apps fall into the non-essential category. This mental inventory naturally fosters a more intentional digital landscape.

Yet, simplifying isn't just about what we remove but how we interact. Examine your relationship with each digital tool you consider essential. Are you using them mindfully, or have they become just another source of noise? It's vital to align their use with your personal values. This introspection helps you move from digital chaos to serenity, turning necessary tech interactions into moments of mindfulness.

Part of this journey is about mindset, embracing a minimalistic philosophy that extends beyond material goods to your digital ecosystem. It's about fostering a conscious experience where you choose to engage, aware and deliberate. The goal is to break the cycle of impulsive usage driven by habit more than intention and create a space where digital interactions enrich rather than overwhelm.

The process of digital simplification also demands periodic reassessment. Technology evolves rapidly, new tools become available, old ones become obsolete, and your own needs shift. Set a schedule, maybe quarterly, to review your digital inventory. Ask yourself if each tool still serves a purposeful role or if there's something better suited to your current life situation.

This process should not be daunting. Approach it as a journey towards peace and clarity. Each step, each tool you deprioritize or delete, creates more room for mental tranquility. Imagine a desktop free of clutter, a phone with only the most functional or joyful apps—a digital life where every interaction is based on choice, not compulsion.

Beyond devices and apps, calm can also be found in saying 'no' to unnecessary digital commitments. How often do you find yourself sucked into group chats that add more stress than joy? Or maybe you're part of mailing lists that clutter your inbox but rarely capture your interest? It's okay to unsubscribe, to leave groups that no longer serve you. In doing so, you create pockets of mental space to focus on what truly matters.

Moreover, simplifying digital interactions extends into the realm of notifications. In the constant ping of alerts, we often lose time we didn't intend to give away. Evaluate which notifications are truly urgent. Maybe your life doesn't need a news update every hour, or instant social media alerts. Prioritize attention for things that matter. Mute or set boundaries for the rest. It's not about being disconnected; it's about being connected more meaningfully.

Don't forget the underlying aspects of digital minimalism—time. Challenge yourself to examine how much time you devote to unproductive scrolling. Utilize screen-time apps not only to track but to impose limits. Adopt practices like setting time blocks for specific digital activities, making it easier to shift offline when needed. This can enhance focus and reduce the anxiety that stems from being perennially available.

Ultimately, simplifying your digital world isn't a one-size-fits-all process. It's deeply personal, reflecting your individual priorities and desires. What matters is to engage in this journey with curiosity and self-compassion. Allow yourself the grace to experiment, fail, adjust, and learn. Progress, not perfection, is the path to harmony between digital life and mindful practice.

As you navigate this path, keep in mind the transformative power of now. Be present with the technology that serves you, and be ever willing to set aside that which doesn't. In doing so, digital minimalism becomes a guiding light, not just simplifying your screen, but invigorating your soul.

Prioritizing Essential Technologies

In our quest for a more mindful digital life, identifying which technologies truly serve us becomes crucial. It's about distinguishing the necessary from the superfluous, allowing us to cultivate a tech environment that supports rather than overwhelms. But how do we decide what constitutes essential technologies? The answer begins with our values and priorities, aligning our tech choices with what genuinely matters to us.

Consider your daily digital interactions: How many of them align with your core values and contribute positively to your life? It's easy to get caught in the whirlwind of new apps and gadgets, each promising to optimize, streamline, or entertain. However, not all technologies offer a meaningful or lasting improvement in our lives. Therefore, we must practice discernment, engaging only with those that uphold our personal and professional goals.

Start by evaluating the impact of your current tech roster. Does your smartphone enhance your productivity and personal connections, or does it distract and drain you? Each device and application should have a clear purpose. For instance, a productivity app may be essential if it genuinely helps you manage tasks and time efficiently. Yet, if it complicates or distracts, it may warrant reevaluation or replacement.

To assist this process, begin by making a list of the technologies you use daily. Group them into categories based on function: communication, work, entertainment, and so on. For each category, question its usefulness and ask if a simpler or more effective alternative exists. This exercise opens up a dialogue between your technological habits and your true needs, bringing clarity to areas once clouded by convenience or habit.

After identifying essential technologies, the next step is designating specific roles for each, ensuring they serve strategic functions. Take, for example, social media platforms. While they can be powerful tools for connection and information, unchecked usage may lead to mindless scrolling. Instead, assign specific purposes like networking, learning, or staying informed about particular interests. This transforms social media from a time sink into a conscious activity.

It's also important to recognize that essential technologies can and should evolve with your life. As your goals change, so too might the tools that best support you. Regularly revisit your tech setups and be open to letting go of what no longer serves you. A new job might necessitate different software; a shift in personal interests might invite new learning platforms. Flexibility ensures your digital environment remains an asset, not an anchor.

Additionally, prioritizing essential technologies involves respecting boundaries and intentions within your digital engagements. Configure your devices to empower rather than interrupt your day. Use "Do Not Disturb" features or app limits that align with mindful practices. These settings are not about restrictions but rather enhancing the quality of your experience, allowing you to be fully present in each moment, digitally or otherwise.

For many, the impulse to upgrade to the latest model or app is strong. Yet, questioning the necessity of new technologies before adoption helps maintain balance. Ask, "Will this truly improve my life?" "Does it align with my current needs and values?" By making decisions through the lens of meaningful enhancement rather than novelty, technology stays in its rightful place—supportive and deliberate.

The process of prioritizing essential technologies isn't about eliminating joy or spontaneity. On the contrary, by curating your digital tools thoughtfully, you create space for what's genuinely important, facilitating more meaningful interactions and engagements. Imagine an artist with a carefully chosen palette, each color serving a purpose. Similarly, each chosen technology should enrich your life, adding dimension and depth, not distraction.

To maintain this balance, incorporate regular digital audits into your lifestyle. Periodically review your tech usage, looking for patterns of complacency or waste, and adjust accordingly. This practice cultivates a habit of mindfulness, reinforcing your intentional relationship with technology over time. As you engage in these retrospectives, you'll likely discover a natural inclination toward less clutter and more clarity.

Remember, the ultimate goal of prioritizing essential technologies is not just efficiency or minimalism for its own sake. It's about fostering a digital life that mirrors your aspirations and supports your well-being. By nurturing a mindful approach to technology, you create a harmonious environment where peace and productivity coexist, enhancing both your digital and personal worlds.

Chapter 7: Mindful Tech Tools

In today's hyper-connected world, technology can either be a source of constant distraction or a beacon of clarity—it's up to us to choose how we engage with it. A mindful approach to tech utilizes specific tools designed to cultivate awareness and promote serenity. Imagine an app that nudges you to take a deep breath every hour or a gadget that filters out digital noise, leaving you with only what truly matters. These tools don't just serve functional purposes; they are allies in your journey toward a more intentional digital life. They're like a gentle reminder, whispering balance into your busy day. By integrating these mindful tools into your everyday routine, you can transform your tech interactions from overwhelming to empowering, paving the way to a harmonious coexistence with the digital realm. You have the power to redefine your relationship with technology, making mindful connections that enrich rather than drain your energy. Discovering and embracing these tools is a step toward not only managing but mastering, your tech-driven world.

Apps for Awareness

In our increasingly connected world, finding moments of quiet reflection amidst the digital clatter can feel like a monumental task. But what if technology could also serve as a conduit to inner peace rather than a cacophony of distractions? Enter apps dedicated to cultivating awareness, which promise to guide users toward a mindful existence in a digital age. These tools aren't just about timing how long you meditate—though that's part of it—but assimilating mindfulness into your daily grind and digital routine.

One of the advantages of using apps for mindfulness is their accessibility. These apps, often rooted in timeless practices, are designed to be intuitive and engaging, seamlessly fitting into any lifestyle. Whether you're at a bustling airport or nestled in a quiet corner of your home, your smartphone or tablet can become a gateway to tranquility. Mindfulness apps come in a variety of forms—each offering different exercises, reminders, and features to keep you grounded throughout the day. With a myriad of options at your fingertips, the challenge often lies in selecting the ones that truly resonate with your intent and needs.

One popular feature found in these apps is guided meditation. For beginners unsure of where to start, guided sessions offer structured and progressive lessons that help cultivate a regular meditation habit. These sessions come in varying lengths, allowing for flexibility regardless of how packed your schedule may be. Whether you have a mere five minutes or a more generous half-hour to spare, there's a session that can be integrated into your day, reminding you that even brief moments can have profound impacts.

Beyond meditation, some apps are equipped with ways to help users incorporate mindfulness into specific activities, like walking or eating. Such features act as gentle nudges, encouraging you to approach daily routines with a fresh perspective, fostering a greater appreciation for the present moment. They can guide you on mindful walks where each step becomes an opportunity to feel the earth beneath your feet, or invite you to savor each bite of a meal with heightened awareness.

Many apps also offer mood tracking and journaling capabilities, enabling you to document emotional shifts and identify patterns over time. Tracking emotions can reveal insights into what triggers stress and joy, empowering you to take conscious control of emotional responses. By tuning into these emotional patterns, users often find themselves better equipped to handle the ebbs and flows of daily life with grace and equanimity.

Community features can enhance the experience, providing a sense of camaraderie and accountability. Some apps allow users to connect with others on similar mindfulness journeys, whether through challenges, group meditations, or sharing experiences. This social aspect can be incredibly motivating, as it links personal growth with a supportive network of like-minded individuals, breaking the notion that mindfulness is a solitary pursuit.

Moreover, many apps integrate reminders and push notifications, serving as periodic prompts to pause, breathe, or simply check-in with yourself. These notifications can be customized—whether it's a gentle buzz every few hours to have a mindful moment or a morning reminder to start your day with intention. They serve as digital cairns, marking opportunities throughout the day to come back to the present, disrupting the autopilot mode that often takes over.

In choosing the right app, it's vital to consider your personal needs and preferences. Some individuals might prefer apps with a minimalistic approach, void of distractions. Others may be drawn to richer interfaces offering elaborate features. Remember, the ultimate goal is to choose an app that invites ease into your practice, not one that adds another layer of stress or obligation.

It's also beneficial to start small. Begin with free versions or trials, exploring what different apps offer before committing to subscription services. Take note of which features you find most beneficial, and allow yourself the freedom to experiment. In doing so, you'll likely discover an app that aligns with both your technical preferences and mindfulness goals.

The underlying beauty of these applications lies in their potential for growth alongside the user. As your mindfulness practice deepens, you may find new ways to utilize these tools, discovering dimensions of self-awareness previously unexplored. This combination of technology and mindfulness is akin to unfolding a map of your inner landscape, with each app serving as a guide and companion in your journey.

Embracing mindfulness through apps does not preclude offline practices. In fact, many find that these apps serve as a scaffold for developing practices that eventually extend beyond the screen. They lay a digital foundation upon which a deeper, more tangible habit of mindfulness can be built, integrating seamlessly into the broader tapestry of mindful living.

The world of mindfulness apps remains ever-evolving, growing as our understanding of digital wellness expands. New features that challenge traditional practices are constantly emerging, ready to meet the needs of an audience yearning for balance. Whichever apps you choose to explore, remember that the ultimate intent is to foster a greater sense of presence and peace within your digital journey.

Through conscious selection and consistent practice, apps for awareness can transform your relationship with technology. They offer the tools not just to survive, but to truly thrive in our bustling digital world—encouraging not just awareness but a life of nuanced attentiveness and intentional being. By embracing these digital companions, the path to a more mindful and connected self is always within touch, elegantly merging the modern with the mindful.

Gadgets That Promote Clarity

Amidst the hum of notifications and the relentless pace of the digital world, a welcome wave of innovation offers a different kind of promise. Instead of accelerating our attention for constant connection, these gadgets are designed to foster clarity and promote mindfulness. It's a new frontier in tech where devices don't just add to the noise but help streamline it, creating pockets of tranquility in an otherwise chaotic landscape. These tools stand at the nexus of technology and mindfulness, implying that peace of mind doesn't always mean stepping away from tech but, rather, interacting with it more thoughtfully.

Imagine a smart pen that not only transcribes your notes into digital texts but also encourages thoughtful writing by limiting your screen time. By bridging the gap between the digital and the physical, it blends the tactile pleasure of writing with digital convenience. Such gadgets echo the sentiment that mindfulness is not about rejecting technology but refining our relationship with it. They serve as gentle reminders to slow down, to take a moment for consideration, and to engage in activities that nurture our mental well-being.

Noise-canceling headphones are a staple for anyone seeking solitude in their sonic environment. Yet, newer models go a step beyond just shutting out the world. Some are equipped with modes that filter in specific sounds to keep us grounded, like the trickle of a stream or the hum of a city's heartbeat, but without the chaos. This feature allows users to create personal soundscapes that reinforce concentration and tranquility, hands down one of the simplest but most effective ways to promote a mindful focus.

Tracking devices like smart rings and wristbands often come under scrutiny for their data collection. However, when used intentionally, they can serve as invaluable guides in understanding our body's rhythms. These gadgets provide insights not just into our physical health, such as heart rate or activity levels, but also our stress levels and sleep patterns. Armed with this data, we can make informed decisions about restructuring our routines to better align with our natural cycles, thereby achieving a potential state of equilibrium.

The dawn of light-based technology brings us to gadgets like sunrise alarm clocks. These devices simulate the gradual rising of the sun to ease users into wakefulness. By mimicking natural light patterns, they help regulate the body's internal rhythms, which can often go haywire due to late-night screen exposure. Such a tech makes waking up a calming experience instead of a jolting ordeal, setting a positive tone for the rest of the day.

Air purifiers with advanced filtering systems are another unassuming gadget that promotes mindfulness by cleaning the invisible clutter that surrounds us—air pollutants. Cleaner air enhances our respiratory health and, by extension, our ability to concentrate and think clearly. A palpable difference becomes apparent as we breathe more freely, a subtle reminder of the benefits of an unburdened environment on our mental clarity and well-being.

Smart watches have evolved beyond mere timekeeping. When linked with mindfulness apps, they serve gentle nudges every hour to pause and breathe, to stretch, or to reflect. This ongoing engagement supports the daily practice of mindfulness in a busy lifestyle, making it accessible and easy to incorporate. It's a digital reminder that doesn't aim to distract but inspire small, meaningful pauses.

As we increasingly seek solace from digital overexposure, the rise of portable sensory deprivation tanks—although a luxury—has also made waves. These resemble private fortresses against the overwhelming stimuli of the modern age. By immersing oneself briefly in such an environment, with zero external input and calming buoyancy, it's possible to achieve a profound level of relaxation and mental clarity that invigorates the mind and body.

In offices and workspaces, standing desks with built-in movement trackers promote physical activity while working. They remind us to change positions, reducing prolonged sedentary periods. This idea goes beyond simple ergonomics, emphasizing how small physical shifts can enhance mental focus and invigorate creative spaces. Strategic movement helps break cycles of monotony and stagnation, nurturing a more dynamic thought process.

The concept of focusing gadgets extends to tools like digital notebooks with e-ink displays that mimic paper without the distractions of full-featured tablets. They provide a convergence of analog and digital, allowing for note-taking without notifications. Such a focused environment breeds creativity and thoughtfulness by limiting the interference common to LCD-based gadgets.

Even the humble timer finds a place on this list, especially those purpose-built for the Pomodoro Technique. These devices, by chunking work into focused intervals followed by brief breaks, help improve productivity and diminishes mental fatigue. They balance work with well-deserved breaks, reminding us that mental clarity is often just a short pause away.

For many, meditation gadgets offer a gateway to mindfulness. Wearable headbands that track brain activity can help users focus by giving real-time feedback on their meditative practice. These modern relics of mindfulness training enhance self-awareness, showing meditation not as an arcane art but as a practical aid for mental clarity in everyday life.

Ultimately, these gadgets find their strength not solely in their technological prowess but in their capacity to anchor us in the present moment. They embody a philosophy that seeking clarity in our digital interactions does not just involve adopting new devices but doing so with intention. By thoughtfully incorporating these tools into our lives, we can leverage technology's potential to enhance rather than hinder our quest for mindfulness. As we continue forward, let these gadgets serve as part of a toolkit—one that promotes clarity, encouraging us to find peace and purpose in the digital age.

Chapter 8: Balancing Work and Digital Rest

In today's world, where remote work blurs the line between professional and personal spaces, finding balance is crucial for maintaining well-being. Setting clear boundaries between work tasks and personal time helps prevent burnout and fosters a healthier relationship with our digital devices. Embracing techniques for digital downtime, such as scheduling device-free periods and crafting intentional routines, can recharge our minds and improve our focus. This isn't just about restricting access; it's about cultivating a sanctuary of rest amidst our burgeoning digital responsibilities. By consciously engaging in these practices, we create a harmonious rhythm that nurtures productivity while honoring the need for respite, ultimately achieving a more mindful and fulfilling digital life.

Setting Boundaries in a Remote World

In our ever-evolving digital landscape, the advent of remote work represents both opportunity and challenge. As borders dissolve and workspaces shift from brick-and-mortar to virtual, the need for setting boundaries has become more crucial than ever. The blurring of lines between professional responsibilities and personal time can lead to an overwhelming sense of connectivity that threatens our mental well-being and work-life balance.

Creating boundaries in a remote world starts with drawing a mental map of your space. Imagine delineating areas where work happens and where it doesn't. This mental demarcation allows you to psychologically step in and out of work mode, even if you're still in the same room. Designating a specific area in your home as your workspace can be immensely helpful, especially if that space mirrors the values of tranquility and focus. Choose a quiet corner with minimal distractions, ensuring it becomes synonymous with productivity and concentration, not a hub of stress.

Time management is another vital aspect of remote work boundaries. Without the physical act of leaving an office, the clock can become irrelevant. Work can encroach late into the night if you let it. Setting specific work hours and adhering to them is critical. It's tempting to mix personal tasks with professional ones during the day, but this often results in a blurred focus. Commit to distinct periods where work takes precedence, and in contrast, grant yourself deliberate moments for digital rest.

Work culture often glorifies the idea of being always available, but perpetual connectivity can severely detract from mindful living. It's essential to communicate these boundaries with your colleagues and supervisors as well. Be transparent about your working hours and your availability for meetings or calls. If you set expectations in advance, you're more likely to have them respected. In the long run, this will aid in cultivating a workplace culture that values well-being and productivity, rather than mere presence.

Beyond scheduling, there's the challenge of digital distraction. Notifications, emails, and messages create a constant hum that can pull you away from deep work or a well-earned rest. Take control by creating systems that support focus and relaxation—either by setting certain times to check emails or by using apps that block distractions for designated periods. Engage with your digital tools, but on your own terms. This helps turn what could be another layer of stress into a means of empowerment.

Besides setting these operational boundaries, emotional boundaries are equally important. Stress from work often seeps into personal life, especially when there's no commute to create a buffer. Creating rituals that help transition from work to rest can aid in this. These could be as simple as changing your clothes, starting a home workout, or engaging in a mindful practice like meditation or journaling. Such activities help signal the brain that work has ended, and personal time has begun, ensuring that both areas of life get the attention they deserve.

Furthermore, the integration of this boundary-setting doesn't imply rigidity. It's about flexibility within a predefined structure, allowing you to meet both personal and professional needs. Assess and adjust boundaries as situations change. If a system isn't working, don't hesitate to revisit your strategies and realign them, ensuring they serve your current circumstances. Reflect on your experiences, noting what aids productivity or peace, and what drains them.

In the remote world, redefining boundaries also involves embracing a mindset of self-compassion. Inevitably, there'll be days when boundaries slip. Projects might require overtime; emergencies may blur the lines. Instead of internalizing this as failure, view it as a learning opportunity and reset with renewed resolve. The goal isn't perfection but creating a harmonious balance that supports your well-being.

This journey isn't undertaken alone. Tapping into support systems, whether through discussions with peers facing similar challenges or seeking guidance from leaders well-versed in remote work, can provide insights and encouragement. Sharing strategies and experiences fosters a community that values mindful, balanced living, promoting resilience in navigating the intricacies of remote work life.

As our world continues to change, setting and respecting boundaries in a remote work environment becomes a vital skill. It is about reclaiming control over our time and mental space, enabling us to engage more wholly both in our professional responsibilities and personal joys. By taking deliberate steps towards establishing these boundaries, we can craft a digital livelihood that thrives amid tranquility and productivity, ultimately leading to a more mindful existence.

Techniques for Digital Down Time

In our hyper-connected world, finding time to disconnect is not only essential but also deeply rewarding. The pursuit of digital downtime might feel counterintuitive in an era where the boundaries between work and personal life have blurred, especially with the pervasive use of smartphones and instant communication channels. However, cultivating moments of digital rest can enhance not only your emotional and mental well-being but also your productivity when you choose to re-engage with technology.

First, let's consider the practice of scheduling technology-free time. Creating designated intervals where you step away from screens allows you to reset and recharge. You might start by identifying specific windows in your day or week where you can be free of digital interruptions. This could be a quiet hour in the morning before your day begins or a restful evening ritual to unwind. By embedding these moments into your calendar, you commit to yourself the gift of disconnection, similar to how you would arrange an important meeting with a colleague.

When planning these breaks, make it a priority to use this time for activities that nourish your soul. Engage in a hobby that requires no digital aid—whether it's painting, cooking, gardening, or reading a printed book. These pursuits remind us of the joys found in simplicity and provide a rich tapestry of experiences away from the digital realm.

Another key technique is the use of digital Sabbath. This involves shutting off all digital devices for a day each week. The concept borrows from the idea of a traditional Sabbath, a time of rest and away from labor, offering you a routine indulgence in peace. Even if a full day isn't feasible, consider shorter periods where digital interactions are significantly minimized, allowing ample headspace to breathe and just "be."

Embracing mindfulness meditation can deepen your digital down time. Techniques like focused breathing or body scans can help center your awareness and curtail the habitual urge to reach for your phone. By integrating these practices into your schedule, you develop a robust mental framework that fosters digital detachment. Try starting with just five minutes of stillness, gradually increasing the duration as it becomes part of your daily rhythm. Apps focused on mindfulness can guide you initially, but aim to internalize these skills until they become instinctive.

Digital boundaries, both physical and psychological, are vital. Allocate distinct spaces in your home for work and relaxation to foster a clear separation between productivity and leisure. If your workspace is defined, it's easier to mentally "leave work" at the end of the day and enjoy digital rest in another room. Similarly, set boundaries with notifications. The constant pinging of alerts can fracture your focus and pull your attention toward your devices even when you're actively trying to step away.

Technology itself can become a partner in crafting your digital downtime. Utilize features like "Do Not Disturb" modes or set app limits on your devices to cut down reliance during certain hours. Implement screen-time monitors that alert you when you've been on a particular app longer than intended. This not only curtails impulsive scrolling but also builds a conscious habit of checking in with your usage patterns.

Communicating your intentions to disconnect is another effective stratagem. Let close family and friends know when you're planning to go offline, ensuring they understand it's an effort to rejuvenate, not an avoidance of interaction. Supportive networks are vital, and sharing these intentions can foster understanding and respect for your endeavors to preserve your mental bandwidth.

Sometimes, stepping outside can be the most fulfilling digital detox. Immersing yourself in nature can rapidly decrease the brain's consumption of overstimulation and restore balance. Whether it's a trail hike, a walk through a park, or simply sitting on a balcony, the act of removing yourself physically and mentally from the digital grind can yield deep restorative benefits.

Lastly, reflect on the implications of your digital usage. Consider journaling about what you gain when you disconnect—the clarity, the peace, the unexpected moments of joy. View digital down times not as deprivation, but as the opportunity to see the world anew and rediscover your sense of wonder. This reflection can reinforce the positive aspects of carving out these spaces, helping you to appreciate the silence amidst the noise.

Adopting these techniques requires patience and practice, but the benefits can profoundly enhance your capacity to live a more balanced, mindful life. As these moments of digital rest accumulate, they invite you to a deeper understanding of both the world around you and your place within it.

Chapter 9: Enhancing Focus in a Distracted World

In a landscape cluttered with endless notifications and digital demands, enhancing focus might feel like an uphill battle. Yet, embarking on this journey offers not only increased productivity but a profound sense of tranquility. To foster sustained attention, it's crucial to establish conscious boundaries that shield your mental space from constant interruptions. By actively minimizing digital clutter, you create an environment where concentration can flourish naturally. Consider embracing single-tasking, where full presence on a single task heightens efficiency and satisfaction. Harnessing deliberate practices such as setting specific goals, utilizing tools for blocking distractions, and incorporating mindfulness techniques can transform how you engage with technology—making each moment purposeful and serene. Remember, your ability to focus is a skill that grows stronger when nurtured with patience and intention.

Techniques for Sustained Attention

In an era where notifications, alerts, and pop-ups are the norm, cultivating sustained attention is not just a desired skill—it's a necessity. Our modern digital environment relentlessly competes for our focus, but with intentional strategies, it's possible to train ourselves to maintain concentration. The journey to enhancing focus in this distracted world starts with understanding the nature of attention itself.

At its core, attention is about choice. Prioritizing one task above others can be challenging, especially when digital marketing and platform algorithms are designed to seduce our focus. Awareness of these external influences is the first step. By acknowledging how our interactions with technology can scatter attention, we're better positioned to reclaim it. Developing sustained attention involves deliberately crafting environments that minimize distractions and foster immersion.

One effective technique is the practice of single-tasking. Despite the pervasive myth of multitasking, our brains perform best when focusing on a single task at a time. Multitasking overloads our cognitive processes, leading to stress and reduced efficiency. By committing to tackle one task with full presence, we engage more deeply and improve the quality of our outputs. Single-tasking embraces simplicity and cultivates a deeper form of engagement.

Creating a distraction-free zone can dramatically enhance focus. Imagine working in an environment where you're perpetually distracted. By configuring our digital tools to reduce interruptions—such as disabling non-essential notifications and using apps that block distracting websites during work sessions—we create a space more conducive to sustained attention. This isn't just about managing the digital, though; it extends to our physical space too. Keeping a clutter-free work area can prevent your mind from wandering to physical distractions.

Mindfulness meditation is another powerful technique for improving attention. Through meditation, we train our minds to notice when attention has wandered and gently bring it back. This practice not only enhances our ability to stay focused but also imparts a sense of calm and reduces stress. With regular practice, meditation heightens our awareness of the present moment, enabling us to engage with tasks more fully and with greater clarity. The serenity that arises from meditation can then spill over into our daily routines, improving overall mood and cognitive engagement.

The Pomodoro Technique is a well-known strategy for maintaining focus over long periods. This method involves working for set intervals—usually 25 minutes—followed by a short break. By breaking down tasks into more manageable periods, we can avoid burnout and maintain high levels of concentration. The short breaks also act as mental refreshers, allowing for a reset before diving back into work. This cycle can keep our minds fresh and focused throughout the day.

Goal-setting is crucial for sustaining attention over time. Clear, achievable goals provide a target for our focus, directing efforts toward meaningful accomplishments. Without such goals, our attention can drift. Setting daily, weekly, and monthly objectives ensures that you're always working towards something concrete, keeping distractions at bay. A well-defined goal is a powerful compass that guides our attention, providing purpose and meaning in our tasks.

Equally important is the practice of self-compassion. It's natural for attention to waver, especially in a world replete with distractions. When it does, rather than chastising yourself, approach the situation with kindness. Recognize the wandering mind without judgment, and guide it back to your task. This practice not only reduces mental friction but also helps build resilience over time.

Incorporating breaks into your routine is key to sustaining attention over longer periods. The importance of breaks can't be overstated. They allow the brain a chance to rest and recharge, which in turn improves productivity and focus. Engage in activities that contrast with your work to re-energize your brain. Whether it's a brief walk, a few minutes of stretching, or even a short session of mindfulness meditation, these respites can invigorate your mind.

Engaging with nature has also shown significant benefits for focus. Exposure to natural elements can reset attention and reduce mental fatigue. When taking breaks, consider stepping outdoors, even if it's just for a short period. The simple act of being in nature, observing its beauty, and breathing fresh air can refresh the mind and enhance attention upon returning to work.

To further help sustain attention, cultivating curiosity can be a game-changer. When genuinely interested in what we're doing, our capacity to concentrate naturally expands. Approaching tasks with a beginner's mind can spark curiosity and engagement, transforming mundane activities into intriguing explorations. This sense of wonder can sustain our focus in the face of potential distractions.

Peer accountability groups can serve as an excellent support system for maintaining focus. Sharing your goals and progress with others can motivate you to stay on track and maintain a level of commitment to your tasks. When others are relying on your updates, it's a powerful driver to keep focused and perform well.

As we become more attuned to the techniques of sustaining attention, it's important to remember that, ultimately, the journey is deeply personal. Each method might resonate differently depending on the individual and their unique environment. It's about discovering what works best for you and fostering a more harmonious relationship with technology. By consciously applying these techniques, we not only enhance our ability to focus but also carve a path towards a more present and fulfilling life.

Reducing Digital Clutter

In an era where every app clamors for your attention, digital clutter poses a significant threat to our ability to focus and live mindfully. It's not just about having too many files; it's the constant notifications, the myriad tabs open on your browser, and the ceaseless pressure to check messages. A life inundated with such digital noise can leave you feeling scattered and unfocused. But fear not: just as you would tidy a physical space to gain clarity, we can and should declutter our digital lives.

Imagine your phone as a clean slate—a device with only the essentials. This may seem utopian, but it's achievable through the careful curation of the apps and functionalities you truly need. Begin by identifying the applications that serve your goals, enhance productivity, or provide essential communication. The rest? Consider them candidates for a digital cleanse. Removing unnecessary apps isn't just a space-saving measure; it's a statement that prioritizes intentional use over habitual engagement.

Notwithstanding their utility, notifications are notorious focus disruptors. They fragment your attention, leading to what is often called "task-switching" rather than multitasking. This disrupts the flow state that is crucial for deep, meaningful work. Customize your notification settings so that only the most critical alerts interrupt your day. For non-urgent matters, set aside specific times to check emails and messages. This approach not only protects your cognitive resources, but also nurtures a more mindful interaction with your digital environment.

Now, let's delve into email management. For many, the inbox is the epitome of digital chaos. Emails tend to stack up, ushering in stress and a sense of being perpetually behind. Implement strategies such as creating folders to categorize messages or using filters to automate organization. Setting fixed spans of time for addressing emails can also mitigate the overbearing impact of an overflowing inbox. By treating email checks with the same intentionality as any other activity, you can foster a less invasive presence of digital communication.

However, digital clutter is not merely about what's on our devices but also how we engage with digital information. Endless scrolling through social media feeds or news articles can serve as a form of escapism, thereby adding to the chaos. Cultivating a mindful online presence means being selective about the information we consume. Be aware of your media consumption habits, and question whether the content aligns with your values and goals. Doing so allows you to reclaim a sense of agency over your digital engagements. Is this really something that needs your attention, or is it part of the chaos that can be put aside?

Cloud storage offers both a blessing and a challenge. While it keeps files accessible and safe, it can also become another venue for clutter if left unchecked. Periodically, take time to organize your digital files. Create logical, hierarchical folders and delete duplicates and outdated files. This not only frees up space but instills a sense of order. By cultivating this practice, you ensure you're surrounded by what is meaningful and necessary.

In a world of perpetual connection, setting boundaries can also reduce digital clutter. Consider implementing digital sabbaths—days designated for minimal screen time. This not only reduces cluttered interactions but allows your mind to refresh, which in turn enhances future interactions when you do reconnect. Much like a clutter-free workspace invites creativity, a break from constant digital influx promotes mental rejuvenation and focus.

Finally, consider the broader implications of a decluttered digital life. A streamlined environment not only facilitates focus, but also impacts your overall well-being. It reduces stress, anxiety, and the mental load associated with keeping up in a hyper-connected world. By curating a purposeful and intentional digital space, you open avenues for deeper mindfulness and presence in both your digital and physical worlds.

Reducing digital clutter is an ongoing journey, an evolving practice akin to mindfulness itself. As with any pursuit of greater awareness and intentionality, the key lies in regular reflection and adjustment. Continually asking—how can this digital tool serve my journey, rather than impede it?—sets the stage for a more mindful relationship with technology. Understanding this, and committing to it, allows technology to harmonize, rather than hinder, in the quest for a more centered, focused existence.

Chapter 10: The Intersection of Mindfulness and AI

As technology evolves, the integration of artificial intelligence (AI) into our daily routines is becoming ever more pronounced. This intersection offers both challenges and opportunities for those seeking to cultivate mindfulness amidst digital landscapes. Mindfulness encourages us to be present, aware, and deliberate in our actions, while AI often operates in the background, shaping our decisions and behaviors in subtle ways. By understanding AI's potential impact on our attention, we can make active choices to incorporate these tools mindfully, harnessing their capabilities to enhance rather than distract from our lives. It's about finding harmony, using AI as a partner in mindful living rather than an interruption. This synthesis of AI and mindfulness doesn't mean rejecting technology; instead, it allows us to embrace it with intention, leveraging AI's power for enhancing our focus and grounding our tech-driven experiences in present-moment awareness. In this digital age, such mindful integration is not only possible but essential for maintaining balance and fostering a sense of tranquility amidst constant connectivity.

Understanding AI's Impact on Attention

Amidst the continuous hum of notifications and a constant stream of information, AI has subtly woven itself into the tapestry of our daily lives. It's evolved into an essential companion, aiding our quest for efficiency while demanding our attention. Yet, the delicate dance between mindfulness and AI raises a profound question: how does AI affect our ability to focus, and what can we do to ensure it enhances rather than diminishes our attention?

At its core, AI has a knack for captivating our attention and often in ways that escape our immediate realization. Algorithms analyze our behavior, predicting what might catch our eye next. They curate personalized content, optimizing it for maximum engagement. This can make productivity flow with ease or, alternatively, drown us in a sea of distraction. For the mindfulness seeker, understanding this dynamic is crucial. It's not about resisting technology but about weaving it into our lives with intention.

Imagine starting your day with an AI-driven assistant suggesting tasks and reminders. The convenience is undeniable, yet the flip side invites a potential overload of stimuli. Our brains, when bombarded with constant inputs, begin to crave novelty, creating a cycle of distraction. This environment challenges our ability to remain present, even as we chase the next digital carrot. Balancing this requires a conscious decision to use AI tools as allies in our mindfulness practice, rather than adversaries.

The intersection of AI and attention isn't just a negotiation of mental bandwidth but a cultural shift in how we perceive communication and downtime. The allure of AI-driven social platforms lies in their ability to foster connection, albeit often superficial, demanding our mental presence in times that might otherwise be reserved for quiet reflection. Here is where the practice of mindful moderation comes into play — embracing AI functionalities that truly add value to our day without overwhelming cognitive domains dedicated to peace and focus.

AI's impact on attention is particularly pronounced when considering the design of smart devices. These devices subtly push notifications, enticing us to respond, thus creating a context where our capacity to single-task wanes. The challenge lies in transforming the "always-on" culture to periods of digital calm. A mindful approach might involve setting boundaries on when and how AI notifications appear, allowing the mind to engage deeply in tasks at hand without frequent interruptions. By doing so, we champion a new digital rhythm that respects attention and fosters mindfulness.

Let's consider the example of workplace environments modernized with AI technologies. Here, the promise of increased productivity can be overshadowed by the risk of fragmentation of attention. AI tools offer real-time insights and performance metrics, but the constant barrage can lead to anxiety and an urgency for continuous availability. By incorporating mindful check-ins and intentional AI usage plans, professionals can regain control, ensuring these technologies serve to enhance creativity and focus instead of splintering them.

In educational settings, AI finds its role as a powerful conduit of personalized learning experiences. The potential for fostering inclusive and engaging learning journeys is enormous. However, students and educators alike must be aware of the seductive lure of AI-enhanced platforms that could lead to cognitive overload. Mindfulness practices, such as setting specific times for using AI tools, can play a pivotal role in maintaining attention while reaping the benefits AI provides.

Moreover, the trajectory AI sets for attention doesn't merely affect mental states but extends to emotional responses as well. The ability of AI to predict and influence user behavior harnesses attention, often subtly nudging emotional well-being. The impact is profound, creating cycles of validation-seeking behavior and potentially heightening anxiety levels. Mindfulness offers a pathway to disentangle these influences, enabling a clearer perception of digital interactions and their emotional weight.

Strategies for harmonizing AI with mindfulness incorporate both technological and personal boundaries. Technologically, it can involve customizing AI settings to filter out noise and streamline essential inputs, promoting a focused environment. On a personal level, nurturing a sense of awareness around AI's role in one's life can instigate intentional engagement with technology, crafting balanced habits that preserve the essence of mindfulness amid digital abundance.

Ultimately, the relationship between AI and attention draws parallels to a balanced diet — everything in moderation. Allow AI to enhance accessibility to information and streamline tasks without letting it dictate the pace of your mental engagement. Adopt a mindful implementation of AI, ensuring technology serves its purpose while allowing space for presence and intentional rest.

The path to digital mindfulness doesn't necessarily veer from technological integration but rather navigates it with wisdom. AI's potential to assist or distract is neutral; it is the lens through which we choose to interact with it that determines its impact. By consciously choosing how we allow AI into our lives, we can build a digital landscape that encourages depth of experience, enriching the intersection of mindfulness and technology.

In essence, AI's impact on attention invites a thoughtful reflection on how we engage with our digital environments. Through mindful practices, we can transform AI from a tool of distraction to one of profound guidance, where it enhances our ability to focus and be present rather than fragment it across countless digital threads. The journey begins with awareness, tempered by intentionality, shaping a future where AI and mindfulness coexist harmoniously.

Mindful Integration of AI Tools

In the rapidly evolving landscape of artificial intelligence (AI), it's crucial to approach technology with a sense of mindfulness. AI tools are becoming ubiquitous in our daily lives, serving purposes as varied as personal organization, entertainment, and professional enhancements. While these tools offer the potential for significant advantages, integrating them mindfully requires careful consideration of how they fit into our personal values and daily routines.

First, let's examine the potential of AI to enhance productivity and focus. AI tools can assist in automating mundane tasks, allowing us to allocate our time and energy to more meaningful endeavors. Take, for example, AI-driven scheduling assistants or email filters; these tools can streamline our work processes and help reduce the clutter that often leads to cognitive overload. Such efficiencies make space for us to engage more intentionally with our tasks, promoting a less frenetic pace and a more mindful presence in our work.

However, the key to mindful integration of AI tools lies in intentional use, not overreliance. It's all too easy to become overly dependent on automation, thus diminishing essential human skills such as problem-solving and critical thinking. To maintain a balance, we should periodically reassess our relationship with these tools. Are they aiding us in becoming more present and focused, or are they becoming another source of distraction? Regular reflection enables us to use technology as a tool for enhancing, rather than detracting from, our mindful living.

AI tools also hold significant promise for personal growth and wellness. Many applications now offer AI-powered meditation guides and mindfulness exercises, seamlessly integrating into our daily routines through personalized suggestions and adaptive learning algorithms. The capacity for AI to provide tailored experiences can foster a deeper understanding of our mental states and aid us in crafting a personalized path toward mindfulness. By analyzing patterns in our behavior and suggesting adjustments, these devices can be our allies in cultivating a life of greater awareness.

Yet, we must remain vigilant about the data these AI tools gather. With every interaction, we provide inputs—data points that paint a picture of our habits, preferences, and even our vulnerabilities. Mindful use of AI necessitates a clear understanding of privacy policies and ensuring our personal information is protected. It's about striking a balance between embracing innovation and safeguarding our autonomy and privacy.

Another aspect of mindful integration is acknowledging the ethical implications of AI. As creators and consumers, it's essential to support the development and utilization of AI tools that align with ethical standards, promoting fairness, accountability, and transparency. This involves questioning who benefits from these tools and recognizing any biases inherent in the algorithms. Mindful integration demands that we not only benefit from AI but also ensure that tech advancements contribute positively to society at large.

Community and collaboration can be enriched through mindful application of AI tools. AI-powered communication platforms can enhance our ability to connect with others more authentically, providing translations and accessibility features that bridge divides. But true mindful integration involves consciously choosing how and when to interact with these platforms. It's about maintaining the human touch in our communications—listening actively and responding thoughtfully while using AI tools as enhancers, not replacements, for genuine interaction.

It's worth acknowledging the role of AI in fostering creativity. Algorithms that once merely replicated existing patterns are now generating novel ideas, compositions, and designs. By partnering with AI tools in creative endeavors, we can expand our own creative capacities. This collaborative creativity can be especially fruitful when pursued with mindfulness, focusing on the process rather than the outcomes, and remaining open to unexpected inspirations and insights.

As we contemplate the mindful integration of AI tools, we should also remind ourselves that the ultimate purpose of these technologies is to serve human needs, not dominate them. By setting clear intentions for their use, we can ensure that technology supports our well-being rather than becoming an unquestioned force in our lives. It is the conscious decisions we make about tech use that transform AI tools into conduits for presence, focus, and intentional living.

Ultimately, the mindful integration of AI proposes a paradigm where technology and human experience converge harmoniously. It invites us to harness the benefits of AI while remaining true to the ideals of mindfulness—awareness, intentionality, and connection. By aligning our engagement with AI tools to these principles, we cultivate a future where technology amplifies our capacity for presence and enriches the human experience with its potential.

Chapter 11: Emotional Regulation Online

In the relentless flow of digital interactions, cultivating emotional regulation online is more than just a skill—it's a necessity for finding balance in our connected lives. As we traverse the landscapes of digital communication, unexpected stresses often arise, leading to emotional turbulence. Fortunately, by combining foundational mindfulness practices with thoughtful digital habits, it's possible to navigate these challenges with poise. The first step involves recognizing when digital stress emerges, allowing us to take informed, calm action rather than reactive responses. Techniques such as pausing before responding to online conflicts or immersing in a brief digital detox can shift our perception, transforming potential stressors into opportunities for growth. By fostering emotional awareness aboard the digital train, we can engage in online spaces with a sense of calm and centeredness, turning the vastness of the internet from a source of conflict into a platform for connection and resilience.

Managing Digital Stress

In our increasingly digital world, managing stress stemming from online activities is a skill vital for emotional well-being. The barrage of notifications, endless streams of information, and constant connectivity can easily lead to burnout if not managed mindfully. But fear not, by integrating mindful practices, one can transform this chaos into a harmonious digital experience.

To start with, it's crucial to recognize the triggers that lead to digital stress. Is it the infinite scroll of social media, the urgency of email alerts, or perhaps the ceaseless digital chatter? Identifying these stressors is the first step toward regaining control. Once aware, the next step is to create personal boundaries. For instance, limiting online time and designating tech-free zones or hours can carve out crucial space for mental relaxation.

Mindful breathing exercises can be invaluable during the online grind. Before diving into work emails or engaging in social platforms, take a few moments to center yourself with deep, conscious breaths. This simple act can significantly shift your mindset from reactive to responsive. With practice, breathing becomes a natural buffer against impulsive reactions online.

Moreover, cultivating a positive online environment is essential. Choose to follow accounts and engage with content that uplifts you. While it's tempting to stay informed by following news sources that offer a heavy dose of distressing updates, balancing this with positive content is necessary for emotional regulation. Similarly, periodically evaluating and decluttering digital spaces, such as your inbox or social media feeds, can diminish the sense of overwhelm and promote a sense of order.

Another effective technique is mindful reflection after online interactions. Spend a few minutes assessing your emotional responses to online engagements. Did certain comments or news articles unsettle you? Analyze why these emotions arose, and consider how you might approach similar situations differently in the future. This practice not only aids in understanding your own emotional patterns but also encourages healthier interactions moving forward.

The power of making digital experiences intentional can't be overstated. Before embarking on any online journey, set a clear purpose for your activities. Are you checking social media to connect with friends or seek inspiration? Identifying your intent helps prevent aimless browsing, reducing exposure to unnecessary stressors. Creating specific goals for online sessions can transform them from potential stressors to purposeful activities.

Pursuing activities that encourage presence over productivity is another strategy. Use mindfulness apps that offer guided meditations or breathing exercises, prompting regular pauses throughout the day. Incorporating such purposeful breaks supports emotional balance, providing a moment to unwind and reset amidst digital duties.

At the heart of managing digital stress lies a community-supported approach. Engage with like-minded individuals who can support your journey toward a mindful digital life. Join online groups centered around wellbeing or mindfulness practices. Sharing experiences and tips fosters a sense of camaraderie and accountability, which can be incredibly motivating.

Adopting mindful consumption habits is an ongoing process rather than a one-time fix. Just as dietary habits need constant attention for physical health, so too does digital hygiene require regular check-ins. Establishing periodic evaluations of digital habits ensures you're consistently aligned with your well-being goals.

Remember, technology is a tool meant to enhance life, not detract from it. By being intentional, setting boundaries, and practicing mindfulness, the digital realm can transform from a source of stress to one of empowerment. Take charge of your online experience, and you'll find not just tranquility, but joy in the connectivity that once overwhelmed you.

Techniques for Handling Online Conflicts

In our interconnected digital world, encounters with conflict have become inevitable. Online spaces offer anonymity and a lack of physical presence, which can sometimes embolden hostile exchanges. However, by mastering the art of emotional regulation, we can transform these interactions into opportunities for growth and understanding. Let's explore a few foundational techniques to handle these conflicts mindfully.

First and foremost, it's essential to cultivate self-awareness before responding to any disagreement. Pause and take a deep breath. Ask yourself why this particular comment or message has triggered an emotional response. Is it because it challenges your beliefs, or does it feel like a personal attack? Often, understanding your own reactions can bring clarity and calmness, making it easier to address the issue without being overwhelmed by emotion.

Another key technique is empathy. Try viewing the situation from the other person's perspective. What is their intention, and what emotion might be driving their behavior? This doesn't mean you have to agree with them, but recognizing their humanity can soften your own response. It's easy to forget there's a real person behind the screen who might be navigating their own challenges.

Once you've grounded yourself with awareness and empathy, strive for open communication. Express your perspective honestly but kindly. Use "I" statements such as, "I feel," or "I believe," rather than "You" statements which can come across as accusatory. This not only helps in conveying your emotions respectfully but also prevents the other person from becoming defensive.

It's crucial to set boundaries, both for yourself and the interaction. If the online conflict escalates to a point where it affects your mental well-being, know that it's okay to disengage. You might choose to mute notifications, step away from the conversation, or even block the user if necessary. Prioritizing mental health and emotional regulation means respecting your limits.

Mindfulness can also play a vital role in supporting these techniques. Incorporating mindfulness practices into your routine can enhance emotional resilience, equipping you to handle conflicts more gracefully. A brief meditation or deep-breathing exercise can shift the focus from the immediate emotional reaction to a more measured and thoughtful response.

For those situations where resolution seems elusive, adopting a problem-solving mindset can be beneficial. Consider what outcome you hope to achieve from the interaction. Is there a mutual understanding to reach, or is it simply about voicing your perspective? Clarity about your goals can guide the conversation towards a constructive resolution.

Moreover, recognize when to involve others. Sometimes, seeking a third-party opinion or mediator can bring fresh perspectives to an impasse. This could be a community moderator or a mutual acquaintance who can help navigate the emotion-laden topic with impartiality and reason.

When emotions run high, taking breaks during heated exchanges allows for cooling off and reflection. A short walk or even stepping away from the device for a few minutes can provide the space needed to regain composure and return to the conversation with renewed calmness.

Finally, learning from every conflict is vital for personal growth. After the dust has settled, reflect on what the experience taught you about your triggers, beliefs, and communication style. This reflection not only contributes to emotional development but also prepares you for future encounters, enabling you to respond with even more grace and mindfulness.

In blending these techniques, handling online conflicts becomes less of a stress-inducing task and more of an opportunity to engage with the digital world thoughtfully. By nurturing awareness, practicing empathy, setting clear boundaries, and embracing mindfulness, each interaction can evolve into a testament of one's emotional maturity and peace. The digital realm, with its infinite connections, holds countless conflicts but also countless chances to grow and transform. With mindful regulation, we can navigate this web with balance and confidence.

Chapter 12: The Role of Digital Mindfulness in Relationships

In an era where digital interactions often replace face-to-face conversations, the need for digital mindfulness in our relationships is greater than ever. It's about finding balance—embracing the connectivity that technology affords us, while also remaining present in our real-world relationships. Practicing digital mindfulness in relationships requires us to be intentional with our interactions, ensuring that technology acts as a bridge rather than a barrier. By consciously choosing when and how to engage with others through digital means, we can nurture deeper connections and avoid the pitfalls of miscommunication that technology sometimes brings. Encouraging moments of undistracted engagement, whether online or offline, fosters trust and understanding. This approach not only enriches personal bonds but also cultivates a shared space of mindfulness within relationships, allowing both individuals to flourish in an interconnected world.

Nurturing Connections Through Technology

In our increasingly connected world, technology is both a blessing and a challenge. It offers ways to foster connections that were unimaginable decades ago yet can also create barriers if not used mindfully. The core of nurturing these relationships through technology lies in balancing connectivity with authenticity. How do we forge meaningful bonds online while preserving the essence of our human connections?

The key to this balance is *intentional use*. By setting thoughtful intentions before we engage digitally, we can transform casual interactions into substantial connections. It's not just about sending a quick text or a funny meme; it's about taking the time to understand the recipient's world, their mood, and their current needs. Sometimes, a well-considered message can speak volumes more than a hastily sent emoji.

One technique to nurture connections is to treat technology as a conduit for dialogue, not a distraction. Scheduled digital meet-ups with friends or family can create a ritualistic sense of closeness. Rather than scrolling through feeds mindlessly, setting aside time for virtual coffee chats or video dinners fosters a structured yet relaxed environment for deeper interaction.

Though technology provides opportunities for constant contact, it can sometimes dilute the quality of our communications. The art of knowing when to balance online conversation with offline presence is crucial for maintaining real-world relationships. For instance, agreeing on 'tech-free' times during in-person gatherings can ensure we are fully present, acknowledging the invaluable connection that eye contact and physical presence bring.

This modern age calls for us to redefine what it means to be 'there' for someone. While a thoughtful message or encouraging comment online can be deeply supportive, it shouldn't replace more intimate gestures, like a handwritten note or a surprise visit. Acknowledging the limits of digital empathy encourages us to complement our online interactions with offline expressions of care.

The hybrid nature of today's relationships demands mindfulness. Platforms designed for communication can do wonders if used correctly. But they can also lead to misunderstandings and conflicts if we're not attentive to the nuances of written communication. Taking a moment before hitting "send" to consider our words' tone and impact can prevent unnecessary misinterpretations.

Embracing technology as an enabler means using it to bridge gaps caused by distance, lifestyle, or circumstance. Whether it's a long-distance friendship or family members living in different states, the digital world lets us maintain and even enhance these bonds through continuous connection and shared experiences. Utilizing tools like shared photo albums, or group video calls keeps our loved ones close, regardless of geographical limitations.

Creating shared digital spaces can foster a sense of community and belonging. Whether it's a family group chat or a shared collaborative project, these virtual spaces can serve as common ground for ideas, support, and storytelling. Here, the technology's role is that of a facilitator—a humble host who sets the stage for connection and creativity, without overshadowing the participants' voices.

Another aspect is the role of etiquette in digital communication. Being polite, considerate, and timely in responding to messages are digital manifestations of respect. This extends beyond words to encompass how we share content, respecting boundaries and privacy preferences. In nurturing relationships, it's vital to ask: Is this the right time or platform for what I want to share? Mindful sharing builds trust and solidarity.

Moreover, technology's potential for fostering inclusivity is immense. For those with physical or geographical constraints, digital platforms offer unparalleled access to maintain social ties and participate in community life. By approaching these opportunities with empathy, we extend our ability to connect beyond traditional limits, celebrating diversity and broadening understanding.

While the digital realm offers substantial benefits, it can easily slip into a source of stress. Learning to disconnect mindfully requires understanding and respecting one's boundaries. It's about recognizing when technology serves our purpose and when it begins to intrude on our well-being. Just as we nurture our physical relationships with attention and care, our digital connections thrive when balanced with self-awareness and intention.

Ultimately, nurturing connections through technology is about embracing its potential while being mindful of its pitfalls. By aligning our digital interactions with our values and needs, we enrich our relationships and enhance our overall sense of connectivity. Technology should be an extension of our humanity, not an obstacle, in the beautiful dance of communication and connection.

Avoiding the Pitfalls of Digital Miscommunication

In our increasingly connected world, the ability to communicate effectively online becomes crucial. Digital platforms have revolutionized the way we interact, bringing benefits such as instant messaging and video calls that bridge geographical distances. Yet, where there's light, shadow often follows. The ease of digital communication carries the risk of miscommunication, potentially fracturing relationships rather than strengthening them. How can you ensure your digital interactions add value, foster connection, and minimize misunderstandings?

One primary issue stems from the lack of non-verbal cues. In face-to-face conversations, we rely heavily on body language, tone, and facial expressions to convey meaning. These elements are lost in text-based communication, creating a space ripe for misinterpretation. A seemingly innocuous message can inadvertently come across as curt or dismissive, due to the absence of tone. To mitigate this, practice clarity in your messages. Instead of brief, terse snippets, aim for communication that is comprehensive, yet concise. Consider prefacing or qualifying statements to provide context where needed.

Meanwhile, emojis and GIFs have emerged as tools to bridge this gap. They inject tone and emotion into your messages, helping to clarify intent and express feelings that words alone might not capture. Over-reliance, however, can trivialize the communication. Use them thoughtfully. They are not a replacement for well-articulated thoughts but a complement to enrich understanding.

Timing is another critical factor in digital communication. The expectation of instant responses can lead to rushed, ill-thought-out messages that increase the potential for misunderstanding. Instead, practice patience both in sending and receiving communication. Take the necessary time to craft your responses, ensuring they're accurate and intentional. Likewise, afford others the grace of time to reply at their own pace, reducing pressure and fostering a more mindful engagement.

The written word - a tweet, an email, a text message - lacks the texture of voice and demeanor. With practice, however, you can cultivate a digital presence that communicates empathy and attentiveness. Active listening in digital contexts involves more than just reading words—it's about engaging with the content and intent fully. Reflective responses, where you paraphrase and query parts of the message, can enhance understanding and show your interlocutor that you value the exchange.

Moreover, digital miscommunication often arises from cognitive biases. Your mood at the time of reading can color interpretations and skew perceptions. If we're stressed, a simple "Can we talk?" may incite unnecessary anxiety. Mindfulness practice can help combat these biases by cultivating presence and awareness. Breathing exercises or short meditations before engaging in important digital conversations can ground you, offering a clearer mind for constructive engagement.

It's crucial, too, to recognize the plethora of communication styles that individuals bring to the digital realm. Some people may be more succinct, while others prefer detailed expositions. Differences in cultural or generational communication styles also play a role. Understanding and adapting to these differences can significantly reduce potential frictions. Seeking clarity rather than making assumptions can prevent small misunderstandings from becoming larger disputes.

Establishing digital communication norms within your relationships can also be beneficial. Discuss preferred communication channels, response times, or code phrases that signal urgency. This transparency helps align expectations and harmonizes interactions. Regular check-ins can further aid this process by providing space for reflection on communication patterns and necessary adjustments.

Lastly, embrace the power of the digital pause. Before reacting, pause to reflect on your emotions and intentions. This is akin to reading a message, absorbing its content, and refraining from immediate response. Such mindfulness not only reduces reactive, emotionally charged replies but also fosters a more thoughtful and earnest communication exchange.

Digital miscommunication is not an insurmountable obstacle. With intention and awareness, your digital interactions can be transformed into clear, meaningful exchanges that enhance your relationships. It's a commitment to mindfulness, tuning into both the subtle and overt signals, continually refining your approach. Through practice and patience, one can turn potential pitfalls into opportunities for deeper connection and understanding.

Chapter 13: Digital Mindfulness for Families

In today's rapidly evolving digital landscape, families often find themselves swept up in a whirlwind of technology, making it challenging to maintain a harmonious home environment. By embedding mindfulness into daily routines, families can foster a sense of balance and presence, cultivating spaces where genuine connection thrives despite the screens. It's about setting intentions for how technology is used, both individually and collectively, and crafting moments where screens don't dominate but rather complement family life. Encouraging mindful media consumption involves not only setting boundaries but also engaging with content that aligns with the values of the family. Through intentional tech practices, families can transform their homes into sanctuaries of calm, where digital tools serve as bridges to deeper understanding rather than barriers. Crafting these mindful habits may require commitment and patience, but the rewards—a more connected, thoughtful, and empathetic family unit—are well worth the effort.

Creating a Balanced Home Environment

In today's fast-paced digital age, creating a balanced home environment has become more critical than ever. Our homes, ideally sanctuaries of peace, have often been invaded by the constant beeps and buzzes of notifications. It's easy to feel overwhelmed when every device clamors for your attention. But balance isn't elusive; it's achievable with a mindful approach. By weaving mindfulness into the fabric of our families' digital lives, we can cultivate a nurturing environment that harmonizes connectivity and calm.

First and foremost, understanding the dynamics of your home is essential. Every family is unique, with its own rhythm and routines. Take a moment to assess how technology fits into your daily life. Is the living room a place for family gatherings or a space where everyone is glued to their screens? Recognizing patterns helps pinpoint areas where change can be beneficial. It's about creating space for genuine interaction, where technology serves the family rather than dominating it.

One of the foundational steps is setting boundaries. Establishing tech-free zones can dramatically shift the energy in your home. Consider designating certain areas or times where devices are off-limits, like during meals or in bedrooms. Once everyone recognizes these zones as sacred, the moments spent together become more meaningful. It's in these unplugged times that families forge stronger bonds, sharing stories, laughter, and even silence, which is golden in its own right.

Additionally, encouraging open dialogue about digital habits within the family is vital. Everyone, from the youngest to the oldest, should feel comfortable discussing their online experiences and challenges. This openness fosters trust and understanding and allows the family to collectively address issues like cyberbullying, screen addiction, or the impact of social media. It empowers each family member to feel supported rather than judged in their digital journey.

Inspirationally, fostering a sense of collective responsibility in maintaining a balanced digital lifestyle can be transformative. Engage the entire family in creating a shared vision of what a healthy digital life looks like. This could involve setting mutual tech goals, such as reducing screen time by a certain percentage or collectively choosing tech activities that bring joy and learning. This collaborative approach not only inspires each member to take ownership but also strengthens familial ties.

Mindful media consumption is another pillar of a balanced home environment. Encourage the family to be discerning about the content they consume and to reflect on how it impacts their emotions and thoughts. Simple practices, like going through each family member's favorite media sources, discussing their content and relevance, can offer insights into their interests and values. It's about nurturing curiosity and discernment, rather than passive consumption, which can enrich the minds of every family member.

Motivating family activities that replace or complement screen time also play a crucial role. Explore hobbies that everyone can enjoy together. Whether it's gardening, painting, or playing music, these shared interests can be a refreshing break from digital engagements and offer a creative outlet. Including outdoor adventures can amplify the benefits, as nature often acts as a natural stress reliever, allowing everyone to reset mentally and physically.

On a practical note, utilizing mindful tech tools can assist in managing digital balance. Plenty of apps and gadgets are designed to promote well-being rather than detract from it. From apps that monitor screen time and suggest breaks to meditation apps that encourage relaxation, these tools can become allies in the quest for a harmonious home environment. Teaching family members to use these tools wisely can further enhance their digital mindfulness.

Setting a mindful example as parents or guardians is perhaps the most powerful action. Children often mimic behaviors they observe, so demonstrating a balanced approach to technology is essential. Show them that it's possible to engage fully with both the virtual and physical worlds without sacrificing one for the other. By living these practices, you instill in them the values of mindfulness and digital well-being that they can carry into adulthood.

Lastly, remember that balance is an ongoing process. It's okay to encounter setbacks or struggle with consistency. Celebrate small victories and continue to adjust strategies as needed. Creating a balanced home environment is a journey, one that evolves as your family grows and changes. Staying flexible and open-minded about these efforts ensures that your home remains a place of restoration and connection amid the noise of the digital world.

Strategies for Mindful Media Consumption

In today's fast-paced digital environment, discovering the equilibrium between connectivity and mindfulness is not just desirable—it's essential. While technology offers incredible opportunities for growth and learning, it also presents challenges that can overwhelm us and our families. How we consume media intricately affects our mental health, attention span, and family dynamics. Thus, it's imperative to adopt strategies that encourage thoughtful media engagement, which not only nurtures our well-being but also enhances family harmony.

Start by setting clear boundaries on media consumption. It's easy to let hours slip away while scrolling aimlessly or binge-watching. Establishing specific times when media use is permitted—like after completing homework or family obligations—helps create structure. Consider designating "media-free" zones in your home, such as meal areas or bedrooms, to encourage face-to-face interaction and limit unnecessary screen time. The dinner table, for instance, can become a sanctuary for meaningful conversation rather than mindless media stimulation.

Mindful media consumption isn't only about time but also about content. Encourage family members to be selective about what they follow, read, or watch. Engage in discussions about the quality and ethos of media content. Are these outlets or channels aligned with your family's values? Instilling a habit of questioning the motives and perspectives of media can foster critical thinking. Share content that inspires, educates, and motivates, thus transforming media consumption into an enriching experience.

Consider the practice of "media fasting." Just as our bodies benefit from brief periods without food, our minds can benefit from digital breaks. A "digital Sabbath," a day or a few hours free from screens, can recharge our mental faculties and strengthen familial bonds. During this time, immerse yourselves in alternative activities like nature walks, board games, or simply talking. These moments act as a counterbalance to the constant stream of digital input.

When re-engaging with media, approach it with intention. Before turning on the TV or opening a social media app, ask yourself, "What am I looking to gain?" Set goals for media engagement, whether it's learning something new, connecting with a friend, or purely entertainment. This intentionality transforms media consumption from a passive activity into an active, purposeful part of your day.

Incorporate practices of mindfulness while using media. Pay attention to physical signs of stress such as eyestrain or restlessness. When browsing online or watching videos, pause frequently to check in with your body and mind. Are particular content or interactions causing anxiety or discomfort? It's crucial to acknowledge these sensations and act accordingly—perhaps by taking a break or altering your activity.

It's also beneficial to cultivate a family culture of sharing and reflecting on digital experiences. After watching a movie or consuming online content, hold discussions that allow each member to express their thoughts and feelings about what they've seen. Reflecting on media together promotes understanding and empathy, allowing family members to support one another in navigating the complexities of the digital world.

Equally important is the concept of "mindful multitasking." Often, media consumption is not singular—it's layered with other activities like eating or working. Strive to practice doing one task at a time, fully engaging in either the media activity or the secondary task rather than fracturing your attention. This discipline enhances focus and reduces the feeling of being overwhelmed.

Consider the role of gratitude in media consumption. Encourage a family practice of expressing gratitude for the positive aspects of media—whether it's educational value, humor, or connection with distant loved ones. This grateful perspective can shift the attitude from viewing media as a mere escapism to recognizing its benefits and creating a more balanced consumption model.

Technology itself can aid in developing a mindful approach to media. Leverage apps and tools designed to monitor screen time and encourage mindful practices. These can provide insights into personal media habits and remind users when it's time to step back. Including the family in these tech-enabled mindfulness efforts can foster a unified approach to healthier media relationships.

Empower each family member to take ownership of their media choices. Encourage kids and adults alike to propose their own rules or challenges to limit media usage and find new hobbies or skills outside the digital realm. Personal accountability can instill a stronger sense of commitment to balanced media consumption.

Finally, remember that mindful media consumption is a journey, not a destination. It's natural for habits to ebb and flow, and what works now might evolve as family circumstances change. Regularly revisit your strategies and be open to adapting them. Engage in ongoing family dialogue about the impact of media on your collective well-being, making adjustments as necessary to maintain harmony.

By adopting mindful strategies for media consumption, families can transform their digital habits into opportunities for growth, connection, and balance. In an era dominated by screens and online interaction, creating intentional and mindful pathways not only enhances personal well-being but also strengthens the familial ties that bind us most intimately.

Chapter 14: Cultivating Creativity with Mindfulness

In a world swamped with constant notifications and digital clutter, finding the discipline to cultivate creativity through mindfulness can seem daunting. Yet, it's often in moments of digital pause that inspiration strikes most vividly. By approaching our digital consumption mindfully, we allow ourselves to harness the boundless potential of the digital world in a way that sparks creativity rather than stifling it. Practicing conscious awareness in online environments encourages us to filter the noise and savor meaningful content, opening pathways for fresh ideas and innovation. Whether you're seeking inspiration or crafting your next big project, embracing a mindful perspective transforms your digital experience into fertile ground for creativity. As you refine your ability to mindfully interact with digital content, you'll not only boost your creative thinking but also develop a deeper sense of tranquility in your digital life.

Finding Inspiration Online

In the swirling sea of digital content, finding inspiration online can feel like searching for a needle in a haystack. Yet, this vast virtual world holds boundless potential for sparking creativity if navigated mindfully. By harnessing the power of intentional online exploration, you can unlock a treasure trove of ideas without falling prey to the overwhelm of information overload. Imagine immersing yourself in a digital landscape that feeds your soul rather than drains it, helping you create with a clarity that mirrors the mindfulness practices you've cultivated offline.

The first step in this journey is setting clear intentions for your online interactions. Before you even open a browser tab or launch an app, take a moment to breathe deeply and center your thoughts. What are you hoping to find or achieve? Perhaps you're searching for artistic inspiration, fresh perspectives, or new skills. Defining your purpose sharpens your focus, transforming what might otherwise be a scattered quest into a meaningful exploration. This mindful approach ensures that your time online is spent in harmony with your creative goals.

Platforms like Pinterest, Instagram, and YouTube become powerful allies when used with mindful selectiveness. Instead of wandering aimlessly, curate your online galleries and subscriptions to align with your passions and interests. Think of these platforms as your ever-evolving inspiration boards, carefully tailored to ignite your imagination. Remember, the algorithms that drive these sites aim to keep you engaged, often by offering more of the same. Occasionally stepping outside your digital comfort zone can introduce you to unconventional ideas and fresh stimuli that might otherwise go unnoticed.

Seeking inspiration online also involves cultivating a sense of presence when interacting with digital content. As you browse through articles, watch videos, or scroll through images, do so with full attention. Engage your senses as if you were experiencing these creative expressions in a physical gallery. Notice the nuances in a photograph, the tone of a singer's voice, or the rhythm in a writer's prose. This heightened awareness enhances your absorption of ideas, allowing you to draw connections and insights that might flourish into something uniquely yours.

While the internet provides a buffet of creative influences, it's crucial to remain vigilant about the fine line between inspiration and mimicry. Mindfulness guides you to process these inspirations into authentic creations rather than carbon copies. Reflect on how different pieces of content resonate with you. What elements spark joy or curiosity? How can these pieces inform your work without overpowering your own voice? Such introspection fosters a creative authenticity that is deeply personal and inherently inspired by mindful engagement with digital content.

Another pivotal aspect of finding inspiration online is participating in digital communities that share your interests. Engaging in forums, groups, or social media circles can introduce you to like-minded individuals and diverse perspectives. Here, the exchange of ideas becomes a dynamic dance of giving and receiving inspiration. These interactions not only enrich your creative toolkit but also your understanding of how others navigate their creative journeys. Approach these communities with openness and empathy, ready to both contribute and learn.

While seeking new content, it's also important to revisit old favorites. There's a certain creative comfort in returning to sources that continually inspire, whether it's a cherished blog, a beloved influencer, or a podcast that always leaves you pondering. These digital touchstones serve as anchors in the ever-changing sea of online noise, offering consistent inspiration and a sense of continuity. They remind you that creativity is not always about the new but sometimes about viewing the familiar through a refreshed, mindful lens.

Maintaining a digital journal can be a companion practice for documenting your online explorations. Use this space to jot down thoughts, links, quotes, or images that resonate during your internet voyages. Reflect on these entries periodically to identify patterns and themes in what inspires you. This practice not only tracks your creative evolution but also ensures that your online explorations translate into tangible outputs in your work. Over time, this journal can become a rich tapestry of digital inspiration woven into your creative fabric.

As you travel through digital realms, it's equally important to set boundaries to safeguard your creative energy. Even the most inspiring corners of the internet can become exhausting if not accessed mindfully. Allocate specific times for online inspiration-seeking, interspersed with offline creativity sessions where the digital is set aside for the tangible. Balancing these worlds nurtures your creative well-being and prevents burnout, allowing your digital explorations to fuel rather than exhaust your creative endeavors.

Candor within oneself is essential in understanding when the digital pursuit of inspiration becomes more of a distraction than a tool. Knowing when to unplug helps in staying true to your creative path. It's in these moments of mindful detachment that ideas often crystallize, growing organically from within rather than forcing them from an external source. Trust in the creative process means trusting that inspiration will meet you again when you return to your digital sanctuary.

Lastly, the concept of digital mindfulness reframes your relationship with technology as a co-creator in your journey. Rather than viewing online explorations as a necessary evil in creative processes, embrace them as opportunities for mindful discovery. With awareness and intention, the internet evolves from a mere tool into a vibrant canvas for cultivating creativity. By practicing mindful navigation, you empower yourself to not only find inspiration online but also to sculpt a harmonious digital presence that enriches both your artistry and inner tranquility.

Mindful Consumption of Creative Content

In our always-on digital age, where creativity and information flow continuously through our devices, it's crucial to pause and nurture our mindful consumption of creative content. This doesn't mean disengaging from the digital world but rather engaging with it thoughtfully. Creativity requires space—not just physical space, but mental and emotional space too. When we're inundated with creative stimuli, we risk losing sight of our own creative selves. By practicing mindfulness while consuming art, music, literature, or even a simple meme, we cultivate an environment where creativity can thrive.

Mindfulness invites us to approach creative content with an open heart and an inquisitive mind. Instead of scrolling endlessly through social media feeds or binge-watching shows, we can choose to be present with each piece of content. This presence is not merely watching or listening but involves engaging with the material in a way that sparks curiosity and introspection. What emotions does it evoke? Does it inspire or provoke thought? Does it resonate with personal experiences or beliefs? By reflecting on these questions, we deepen our interaction with creative content and connect more profoundly with both the creator and the art.

Moreover, mindful consumption acts as a filter through which we can discern the kind of content that enriches our creative lives versus what drains it. When faced with endless options for media consumption, it helps to be selective. Identify what aligns with your creative goals and values, and what's just noise. This does not mean shying away from challenging content that pushes boundaries or comforts you—it means choosing content that supports your personal narrative or expands it in meaningful ways. When applied consistently, this method curates a digital experience that both informs and enriches one's life.

Paying attention to the intent behind content creation also forms a part of mindfulness. Creative works can be transformative when they carry intention—whether to entertain, educate, provoke thought, or inspire action. As consumers, recognizing this intent helps us appreciate creativity's multifaceted nature. We can honor an artist's perspective while contemplating our unique responses. A mindful engagement process might also encourage dialogue—a conversation with friends, a commentary discussion online, or even a personal musing in a journal—which allows for a richer and more nuanced understanding.

While the internet is a repository for all forms of creative expression, nurturing creativity requires more than just consumption—it requires creation. Inspiration from mindful consumption often leads to a bedrock of ideas ready to be molded into our own creations. Following a mindful engagement with content, let your creativity flow. This transformation occurs when the inspiration received translates into writing a story, painting a picture, crafting a piece of music, or any other form of personal expression. This output enriches the creative cycle, benefiting both the creator and the audience.

Sometimes, the sheer volume of available content creates pressure to consume more than we're ready for. It's easy to fall into the trap of measuring cultural engagement by quantity rather than quality. Mindfulness counters this by encouraging us to digest content slowly, pausing to savor each bite. Like appreciating a fine meal, we should not rush the experience. This tempered and intentional approach allows for the digestion of complex ideas and appreciation of subtle details, which a hurried consumption might overlook.

Adopting mindfulness in creative consumption becomes transformational when focused on how it influences our emotional state. Content carries with it emotional charges and spectrums, impacting our mental well-being. Mindfulness encourages us to recognize these emotional responses. Whether it brings joy, sadness, inspiration, or agitation, acknowledging our emotions can guide future consumption decisions. If certain content continuously invokes negative feelings, it might be beneficial to reassess its place in your consumption patterns. The goal is to cultivate content that uplifts and enriches, complementing inner peace rather than disrupting it.

Incorporating regular reflections on how content impacts creativity and mindful living can steer our digital practices towards a balanced life. It's beneficial to equate this process with regular check-ins. How does the consumed content affect your creative output? Has it influenced your perspective or your mood? The answers will likely evolve as the media landscape shifts, but maintaining awareness equips you to adjust thoughtfully.

Lastly, sharing and discussing creative content mindfully can forge deeper connections with others. Dialogue rooted in mindful consumption isn't merely an exchange of opinions—but rather a collaborative exploration of ideas. Engaging in conversations that celebrate diverse interpretations and experiences can lead to a broader understanding of creativity's impact on life. It transforms solitary digital experiences into shared human experiences, fostering community and belonging.

The practice of mindful consumption of creative content ultimately harmonizes our tech-driven lives with our need for creativity and connection. By approaching digital experiences with openness, selectivity, reflection, and curiosity, we can nurture our creativity and maintain a balanced relationship with the infinite streams of content. As we navigate this digital terrain, let mindfulness guide us in choosing pathways that illuminate and elevate our creative essence.

Chapter 15: Mindful Data Consumption

In an era where data bombards us from every direction, cultivating a mindful approach to information is both a challenge and a necessity. Mindful data consumption invites you to slow down, engage your critical thinking skills, and choose how you interact with news and information sources purposefully. This means discerning credible content, questioning biases, and seeking diverse perspectives to develop a well-rounded understanding of the world. It's about transforming the overwhelm into intention, letting go of the reactive urge to consume indiscriminately, and fostering a deliberate relationship with the digital content we encounter. By doing so, you can cultivate a more reflective and balanced digital experience, where you're not just passive recipients of information, but active participants in what you choose to let into your mind and life. Such mindful engagement with data leads not only to personal tranquility but also to a more informed and conscious society.

Navigating News with Awareness

In an era where news is as omnipresent as air, maintaining a mindful approach to its consumption can feel like navigating a labyrinth. We're bombarded with headlines and stories through every conceivable channel, each vying for our attention. But amidst this deluge, how can one remain both informed and at peace? The answer lies in mindfulness—approaching news with awareness, discernment, and intent.

The first step in navigating news with awareness is recognizing the sheer volume and the constant flow of information. Acknowledge the intensity of modern media but don't let it overwhelm you. It's easy to get swept away by the tide of breaking news notifications and social media updates. So, make a conscious decision to create boundaries around when and how much news you consume. Perhaps, designate specific times in your day for news-checking rather than allowing it to interrupt you at any moment. This simple change can significantly reduce anxiety and create mental space.

Moreover, it's crucial to cultivate critical thinking skills. Not all news is created equal, and being mindful requires you to evaluate the information critically. Ask yourself: Who's reporting this? What's the source's credibility? Is there an underlying bias? By considering these questions, you increase your control over the information's effect on you. This approach turns a passive habit into an active choice, empowering you to become a more discerning news consumer.

Another essential aspect is emotional awareness. News is designed to provoke reactions—it can evoke fear, anger, joy, or despair. Being aware of your emotional responses is vital. Take a moment to observe how certain stories affect your mental and emotional state. Does a specific narrative leave you feeling agitated or even helpless? This self-awareness allows you to step back and process your emotions logically, rather than letting them spiral. Ponder whether your emotional response aligns with your core values and adjust your engagement with sensational news accordingly.

Integrating this mindful practice with news also means embracing the concept of digital minimalism—curating your newsfeed to suit your needs and well-being. Follow trusted sources and limit your exposure to content that doesn't serve your peace. You don't need to know everything that happens in every corner of the world. Prioritize quality over quantity, depth over breadth. This selectiveness is not about ignorance, but rather about preventing information overload.

Additionally, consider the power of slow news. While our culture often prioritizes immediacy, there's much to be said for engaging with longer, insightful pieces that provide context and deeper understanding. Such articles foster a more grounded comprehension of events, unlike the short, rapid-fire updates that dominate our feeds. Just like savoring a well-cooked meal, thoughtful reading can satisfy intellectual appetite and nourish the mind.

Mindful news consumption also involves recognizing and respecting personal boundaries. Engage with the avenues of news that align with your interests and values, but don't hesitate to protect your mental health by disengaging when necessary. If a particular topic or story becomes overwhelming, it's entirely acceptable to step back. Self-care is a vital aspect of mindful living, and that includes controlling your news intake.

Sharing news mindfully is another practice to consider. When you come across a piece of information that's worth sharing, take a moment to reflect on its potential impact. Is it uplifting or could it negatively affect others? News spreads rapidly in our digital age, and being a conscious bearer of information means considering these effects. In this way, mindfulness extends beyond your personal consumption and into the broader community.

Guided meditation or mindful breathing techniques can also prove invaluable in maintaining equilibrium while navigating the news. These practices promote detachment and help prevent the news from hijacking your emotions. As you read or watch, take moments to engage in deep breaths or brief meditation breaks to recalibrate your focus and maintain a sense of tranquility.

In essence, approaching news with mindfulness is a commitment to continuous reflection and adaptation. It's about integrating awareness into every aspect of news consumption— from the moment you select a source to the time you close a news app. By actively deciding when, what, and how you engage with news, you reclaim your agency over your digital experience. This mindful navigation not only fosters calm but enriches the quality of the information you choose to let in.

As we harmonize our digital lives with mindful practices, the process of consuming news becomes a mindful activity that respects our inner peace and seeks to enrich rather than overwhelm. News, after all, should inform and enlighten, not dominate or diminish our well-being. By adopting these mindful strategies, we cultivate a sense of clarity that ensures our engagement with the world remains both conscious and compassionate.

Evaluating Digital Information Critically

In a world inundated with information, the ability to critically evaluate what we encounter online has never been more vital. It's not just about access anymore; it's about discerning which pieces of the vast digital landscape merit our attention and thought. To engage in mindful data consumption, we must embrace strategies that sharpen our critical thinking and enhance our decision-making abilities, leading to a more intentional and peaceful interaction with technology.

The first step to evaluating digital information critically is recognizing the prevalent issue of misinformation and its impact on our perception. The digital age has democratized information sharing but has also blurred the lines between credible sources and those with questionable motives. Understanding this landscape requires vigilance and a commitment to questioning the validity of the information presented to us. It's about asking the right questions: Who is the source? What is their agenda? Is this information corroborated by other reliable sources?

Consider the importance of context. Much of the content we consume online is designed to elicit strong emotional responses—anger, joy, fear, or even passion. By recognizing the emotional pull of these narratives, we can pause and reflect before engaging further. Mindfulness teaches us to stay present and avoid immediate reactions. This awareness aids in distinguishing emotional manipulation from genuine information, giving us the space to process thoughtfully rather than impulsively.

Imagine a digital ecosystem where every click or share is a mindful choice. Here lies the potential for developing a habit of intentional skepticism. This is not to breed cynicism but to cultivate a healthy sense of inquiry. Encouraging ourselves to say, "I need to know more about this," fosters an environment where informed decision-making thrives. It requires us to seek out diverse perspectives and not settle for the first piece of information that aligns with our pre-existing beliefs.

Moreover, reevaluating our engagement with social media can aid in our pursuit of critical thinking. Social platforms, designed to reward quick reactions, can trap us in cycles of surface-level engagement. Embracing silence before responding or spreading information can be transformative. Engaging with the content mindfully can mean moving away from commenting in haste to reflecting on whether our engagement is truly warranted and beneficial.

Mindful data consumers also understand the value of cross-referencing information. In practice, this means making use of multiple sources, looking for consistency, and identifying consensus among experts or reputable outlets. It's vital to become familiar with the strengths and weaknesses of various media. Peer-reviewed articles, expert opinions, and data from reputable institutions often provide a more stable foundation than opinion pieces or user-generated content.

The role of technology itself in our critical evaluation processes shouldn't be overlooked. Algorithms influence what shows up in our feeds, shaping our perceptions of reality. Are we aware of these algorithms, and do we understand how they work? Mindfulness here involves tracking the way personalized content can create echo chambers that affirm our biases, limiting our exposure to new ideas.

Imagine navigating your digital world equipped with a toolkit of questions and a mindset rooted in openness rather than defensiveness. This approach doesn't just protect against misinformation but also enriches the way we engage with and perceive the world. By evaluating digital information critically, we are not merely filtering out noise but carving out a space for clarity in an otherwise overwhelming digital landscape.

This journey is deeply interconnected with a larger understanding of mindfulness. Where mindfulness teaches us to see without judgement, critical evaluation trains us to think without assumptions. Together, these practices empower us to participate in digital spaces more judiciously. They highlight the importance of balance between skepticism and open-mindedness—finding that sweet spot where inquiry meets discernment.

To develop these skills further, consider leveraging educational resources and tools that hone critical thinking. Online courses, workshops on media literacy, or even discussions with others committed to mindful consumption can enhance your skills. Engaging with these mediums enables us to dissect information effectively and develop a nuanced understanding of the content that dominates our screens.

Critically evaluating information requires dedication, patience, and practice. It embraces the notion that while the digital world offers endless streams of content, not all of it deserves a place in our minds and lives. Our goal becomes filtering with care, focusing on what truly enriches our understanding, and aligning our information consumption with our values and intentions.

Our engagement with digital information is, ultimately, a reflection of our internal states. As we cultivate mindfulness in our lives, the process of evaluating information becomes a natural extension—an opportunity to practice patience, show restraint, and value quality over quantity. Through this practice, not only does our relationship with technology transform, but so does our capacity to connect more deeply with the world around us.

Chapter 16: Harnessing Virtual Reality for Inner Peace

As we continue to navigate our technology-driven existence, a new frontier offers unexpected tranquility: virtual reality (VR). This powerful tool, once synonymous with gaming and escapism, is now being harnessed to foster deep inner peace and mindfulness. Imagine slipping on a VR headset and finding yourself instantly transported to serene landscapes designed for meditation. These immersive worlds can gently guide you to a state of calmness and relaxation, offering a sanctuary from the relentless digital noise. As you engage with these environments, VR can help anchor your attention, enhance your meditative practice, and promote a profound sense of presence. By embracing this cutting-edge technology with mindful intent, we can transcend our physical limitations, exploring boundless possibilities for inner peace. Just as we skillfully choose apps and gadgets for clarity, virtual reality emerges as a guide toward serenity in our digitized lives, hinting at an innovation-filled future for mindfulness practices.

Applications of VR for Meditation

As technology evolves, it brings with it a potential for new dimensions of mindfulness, offering pathways to peace in the digital age. Virtual Reality (VR) is one such pathway, transforming meditation practices by immersing users in environments crafted for tranquility and introspection. For the overwhelmed individual seeking serenity away from continuous connectivity, VR serves as a sanctuary—a digital retreat where distractions fade into oblivion. Imagine stepping into a world where the cacophony of daily life is replaced by the gentle lapping of waves or the hush of a forest at dawn. This is the promise of VR meditation, a tool not only for escapism but for genuine therapeutic value.

VR offers immersive environments that enhance traditional meditation techniques, engaging multiple senses to cultivate presence and focus. Traditional meditation may pose a challenge to beginners, as it requires one to sit quietly and turn inward amidst the incessant stream of thoughts. However, VR's vivid landscapes can draw the user into a meditative state more naturally, guiding them gently into introspection. By experiencing a virtual temple, a serene beach, or even the vast expanse of a starry night sky, one can cultivate mindfulness with greater ease and intention. The beauty here lies in VR's ability to adapt and respond to our needs, offering a custom experience tailored for calmness and clarity.

Furthermore, VR can significantly aid in specific meditation practices, such as guided visualization, by providing context-rich, sensory experiences that deepen engagement. Users can follow a voice as it narrates a journey through a breathtaking valley or a tranquil forest, feeling as though they're truly traversing the terrain. This level of immersion can be profoundly effective for visualizations intended to inspire peace, heal turbulent emotions, or foster self-compassion. The virtual surroundings can act as powerful visual anchors, pulling users deeper into a state of meditative absorption.

Another exciting aspect of VR meditation is biofeedback integration, where the technology can respond to the user's physiological state in real-time. Headsets equipped with sensors can monitor stress indicators like heart rate or galvanic skin response, altering the virtual environment to promote deeper relaxation. If stress is detected, the environment could automatically adapt—perhaps transitioning from a desert-scape to a placid mountain stream. This creates a personalized and dynamic experience, uniquely attuned to the user's emotional and mental landscape.

For those new to meditation, VR provides an engaging and practical introduction, breaking down the barriers that often deter people from continuing their practice. With guided sessions and intuitive applications, individuals can learn how to tune into their breath, observe their thoughts without judgment, and develop a sense of presence. Beginners often find it difficult to maintain practice consistency; VR offers a compelling reason to return to their meditation routine, as the experience itself becomes a reward, gradually shaping meditation into a habit.

Experienced meditators also benefit from VR's capabilities by exploring new layers in their practice. The nuanced visual and auditory cues not only add depth to familiar techniques but can also challenge seasoned practitioners to advance their mindfulness skills further. With VR, one can venture into meditation paradigms less accessible before, such as the experience of deep space or the ocean's floor, which would otherwise be impossible to achieve in the physical world. These experiences can lead to profound insights and expanded awareness, fostering growth on a spiritual level.

Communal VR meditation sessions could redefine the meaning of meditating in a group setting, allowing people from different locations to share a unified experience. Virtual group meditations can simulate sitting sessions in temples or mindfulness centers without geographical constraints. Participants can gather in a shared virtual space, fostering a sense of community and connection across vast distances. As individuals harmonize their breaths in unison, despite being continents apart, technology serves as an enabler for global collective consciousness—a testament to VR's potential to unify rather than isolate.

The application of VR in meditation also opens possibilities for targeted therapeutic interventions. Individuals dealing with anxiety or PTSD, for example, can access specialized VR programs developed to provide healing and relief from symptoms. Therapeutic VR experiences can encourage safe exposure to challenging scenarios in controlled environments, helping users to gradually build resilience and strength. This personalized approach not only enhances therapy outcomes but empowers users to actively participate in their healing journey.

Nonetheless, the integration of VR into meditation comes with considerations. Ensuring that the technology supports rather than distracts from mindfulness is paramount. As enticing as VR's allure can be, it should complement traditional practices rather than replace them. It is vital to remain aware of potential downsides, like over-reliance on technology for peace, inadvertently adding layers of complexity to a practice meant to simplify and declutter the mind.

Ultimately, the application of VR for meditation reflects the endless possibilities technology offers to those seeking balance in a hyper-connected world. Whether it's providing a gentle nudge to beginners, enriching the practice of seasoned meditators, or delivering effective therapeutic interventions, VR stands as a beacon of calm amidst the digital storm. As we forge ahead, blending ancient mindfulness wisdom with cutting-edge technology becomes the key to paving a path of inner peace—where the virtual and the mindful coexist harmoniously, nurturing tranquility within the digital realm.

The Future of VR Mindfulness Practices

The realm of virtual reality (VR) holds remarkable potential for enhancing mindfulness practices as technology advances. While VR has often been associated with gaming and entertainment, its capability to transform mindfulness cannot be understated. By offering immersive experiences that feel real, VR allows individuals to transcend the physical limitations of their environment and explore a world built for mental peace and calm. For those feeling overwhelmed by constant connectivity, VR offers new pathways to tranquility by providing a sensory-rich escape from the chaos of daily life.

Imagine a serene beach where the waves rhythmically wash ashore, or a peaceful forest filled with the sound of rustling leaves and chirping birds. VR can create such environments with a sense of realism that screens and headphones alone can't match. These environments can naturally facilitate meditation by making it easier to focus and center oneself, enhancing the ability to be present. As users wear a headset and are visually and audibly transported to these peaceful worlds, they can practice guided meditations tailored to the VR environment, creating a seamless fusion between technology and mindfulness. The fusion promises to engage multiple senses, offering a deeper, more holistic experience of mindfulness than previously possible.

The adaptive nature of VR also means mindfulness practices can be personalized to cater to individual needs. VR mindfulness applications could analyze a user's behavior and preferences, adapting the meditative journey in real-time. For example, someone who finds peace in nature might enjoy virtual landscapes, while another person might be drawn to abstract shapes and colors. This customization ensures that mindfulness practices are not one-size-fits-all, but rather unique experiences that cater to various paths towards tranquility.

As technology continues to evolve, we can foresee the development of social VR environments for mindfulness. These spaces could offer collaborative meditation experiences where individuals worldwide can come together in a shared environment to meditate, practice yoga, or simply relax. Such social VR spaces would dissolve geographical barriers and create communities centered around mindfulness, fostering connection and support among individuals who seek similar paths to inner peace.

Moreover, VR could potentially enhance biofeedback techniques by integrating sensors that monitor physiological responses. With such technology, users can receive immediate feedback on their state of relaxation or stress levels, encouraging self-awareness and regulation. By observing changes in their virtual environment in response to heart rate or breathing patterns, users could learn to better control their physiological state, leading to improved emotional regulation and a more profound engagement with mindfulness.

The advances in VR technology also bring new challenges, primarily involving accessibility and affordability. As with many technological innovations, VR equipment can be expensive, and its effectiveness in mindfulness practices may initially be limited to those who can afford it. Ensuring the accessibility of VR for mindfulness purposes is crucial for it to be widely adopted and integrated into daily life. Potential solutions could include creating more cost-effective devices or developing partnerships with mindfulness organizations to make VR sessions available in community centers or online platforms.

Another consideration is the potential for overreliance on VR for mindfulness and the necessity of maintaining a balance between virtual and real-world practices. While VR offers unique opportunities to enhance mindfulness, it should complement, not replace, traditional mindfulness practices. Engaging in mindfulness without any technological aids will remain essential for grounding oneself in the present moment as these practices are effortlessly integrated into daily life.

The future of VR mindfulness practices is also intertwined with ethical considerations. Privacy and data protection must be prioritized as VR applications could collect sensitive biometric data to enhance user experiences. Trust and transparency in data handling and storage will be essential to ensure users feel secure when engaging in such practices. Developers and policymakers must work closely to establish frameworks that protect individuals while enabling the benefits of VR mindfulness.

Finally, the potential for VR to democratize mindfulness and make it more accessible is significant. Traditionally, accessing mindfulness teachings required certain resources or specific places—be it classes, retreats, or guidance from a mentor. VR has the power to bring these transformative experiences to anyone with an internet connection and a headset, allowing mindfulness to be practiced on-demand and in diverse settings worldwide. As VR continues to develop, it may help bridge gaps in mindfulness education, offering users an accessible and interactive means of engaging with inner peace, regardless of their surroundings.

As we peek into the future of VR mindfulness practices, the possibilities for deepening and democratizing these practices are both vast and inspiring. The convergence of mindfulness and VR has the potential to not only offer inner peace but also to innovate how we interact with, understand, and enhance our mental well-being. As mindful living increasingly integrates into digital life, VR stands as a promising frontier for personal growth, connection, and serenity.

Chapter 17: The Workplace Zen

In the hustle and bustle of modern work life, finding a moment of peace can feel like searching for a needle in a haystack. Yet, incorporating mindfulness into your daily professional routine can transform this chaos into calm. Imagine starting your day with a few deep breaths, allowing your thoughts to settle before diving into emails and meetings. Simple practices like these create a protective shield against stress, aligning productivity with personal well-being. Embrace setting boundaries for digital communication, and witness how focused intention makes room for genuine creativity and collaboration. By taking control of your environment and embracing moments of stillness, you hit the reset button, paving the way for both success and serenity in a digital world that never seems to sleep. Balancing professional demands with inner tranquility isn't just possible—it's essential for thriving in today's ever-connected workplace.

Mindful Practices for Professional Success

In a world where emails ping almost as often as our heartbeats, finding professional success while maintaining a sense of calm can feel like a Herculean task. Yet, it doesn't have to be. In the midst of deadlines and meetings, mindful practices can become a lighthouse guiding us through the stormy seas of digital demands. They can help not only in enhancing productivity but also in fostering a deeper sense of satisfaction in our work.

The notion of mindfulness in the workplace isn't merely a fleeting trend—it's a vital tool for those seeking to harmonize efficiency with well-being. Picture this: you're facing an avalanche of tasks, and instead of feeling overwhelmed, you're able to zero in on each task with clarity and purpose. This isn't just a pipe dream. Through mindful practice, it's possible to cultivate an environment where calmness and productivity coexist.

For many, the first step toward mindfulness at work is simply breathing. It sounds almost too simple, yet the simple act of conscious breathing can reset your mental state. Taking a few moments to focus solely on your breath can silence the mind's chatter and bring you into the present moment. Try integrating short breathing exercises between tasks or before meetings. Over time, these moments of stillness can profoundly influence your professional demeanor.

Consider also the practice of setting intentions at the start of your day. While to-do lists prioritize tasks, intentions can prioritize the type of day you wish to have. By deciding to approach challenges with curiosity over frustration, or meetings with attentiveness rather than distraction, you ignite a mindful perspective. Many professionals find that writing down a daily intention helps to anchor their focus and acts as a touchstone when the day turns chaotic.

Incorporating periods of stillness into daily work routines can encourage a healthier mental state. For instance, individuals embarking on a work project may benefit from periodic pauses. These planned breaks create space to reflect, recalibrate, and return to work with renewed vigor. Unlike endless hustle, mindful pauses encourage efficiency as they allow the brain to rest and regenerate.

The digital nature of today's work environment can also cause a sense of disconnection. Mindful practices urge us to reconnect with the human aspect of work by engaging deeply with colleagues. Active listening during meetings and interactions helps foster clearer communication and stronger relationships. Making a conscious effort to fully engage with whoever is speaking, putting aside distractions, can show colleagues that their words are valued, often leading to more meaningful exchanges and collaborations.

By being fully present in meetings rather than being tethered to smart devices, leadership skills can manifest organically. Colleagues appreciate being heard and understood, strengthening team cohesion. This level of attention and presence doesn't just benefit professional relationships—it can also transform organizational culture.

Another beneficial practice is to create a workspace that encourages mindfulness. Whether you're remote or in an office, your work environment plays a significant role in shaping your mental state. Decluttering, incorporating elements of nature, and personal touches can make your workspace a sanctuary. This nurturing environment can reinforce a sense of peace and focus, turning the mundane into moments of beauty.

In terms of workflow, consider adopting techniques such as the Pomodoro Technique, which promotes short, focused work periods followed by breaks. Such structured time management can stave off burnout and enhance concentration. When distractions fight for our attention, these practices remind us to honor our limits.

It's essential, too, to acknowledge when gratitude can be woven into your routine. Gratitude doesn't entail ignoring challenges but rather recognizing what goes well amidst them. Taking time to jot down or silently acknowledge appreciations at work can boost morale and decrease stress. Gratitude shines a light on positivity and reshapes how we perceive our work life.

Ultimately, these mindful practices serve as a foundation for building resilience. They equip you with the toolkit needed to handle professional hurdles with grace. Embracing imperfection, forgiving missteps, and viewing them through a lens of growth—not as failures—can cultivate both empathy and perseverance in a professional context.

In concluding this section, recognizing that success is not solely defined by outcome but by the journey itself can be liberating. Mindful practices allow professionals to redefine what success looks like, focusing on holistic progress and meaningful engagements. In doing so, they contribute to a truly fulfilling career path, balancing achievements with overall well-being.

Balancing Productivity with Wellbeing

Achieving a balance between productivity and wellbeing in today's digital age is akin to walking a tightrope. It's a challenge that many face as our work environments continually evolve, pushed by advancements in technology that keep us tethered to our devices. Yet, finding this equilibrium is not only possible; it's essential for maintaining a healthy and fulfilling professional life. The key lies in integrating mindful practices into our daily routines, allowing us to leverage technology without being consumed by it.

We often assume that being busy equates to being productive. However, being perpetually occupied can lead to burnout rather than actual accomplishment. It's crucial to differentiate between tasks that are genuinely valuable and those that merely add to the noise. Mindfulness helps us identify what truly matters by encouraging a process of reflection before action. By taking a moment to breathe and assess the importance of each task, we can prioritize effectively and focus our energy on what yields the greatest results.

The impact of constant connectivity is more profound than we realize, often manifesting as increased stress levels and decreased overall wellbeing. Acknowledging this is the first step towards change. Implementing digital boundaries can significantly enhance our mental space. Setting specific times for checking emails or engaging in work-related communications helps create a clear division between work and personal life. This intentional limitation reduces the impulse to react immediately to every notification, thus fostering a controlled and relaxed environment.

However, establishing boundaries is only one piece of the puzzle. Embracing mindfulness in the workspace means incorporating techniques that promote peace and clarity amidst tasks. Simple practices like deep-breathing exercises or short meditation breaks can act as powerful tools to reset our minds, offering moments of tranquillity that refresh our focus and enhance our productivity. These practices remind us that quality often surpasses quantity when it comes to work output.

Moreover, the physical environment plays a crucial role in supporting our wellbeing. A clutter-free workspace aids in maintaining a sense of calm and order. Organizing our digital tools and files helps prevent the confusion that often accompanies a scattered digital life. This, in turn, facilitates a smoother workflow and a clearer mindset. Investing the time to declutter periodically can improve not just the aesthetics but also the functionality of our workspace, making it more conducive to productivity and creativity.

Collaboration and communication are integral components of modern workplaces, yet they can sometimes hinder rather than help if not managed mindfully. It's important to ensure that meetings are purposeful and efficient. Setting clear agendas and expected outcomes can prevent unnecessary time consumption and promote meaningful discussions.

Additionally, adopting active listening during team interactions can enhance understanding and foster a supportive work environment.

Mindful technology use also involves recognizing when to disengage. The human brain wasn't designed for constant stimulation, and without conscious breaks, both productivity and creativity can suffer. Scheduling regular intervals of digital downtime helps recharge our cognitive resources. These moments don't have to be lengthy—a few minutes of stretching or a brisk walk can significantly impact our cognitive rejuvenation, restoring our energy and reducing fatigue.

Equally, it's vital to understand the ebb and flow of our personal productivity rhythms. Identifying peak times of motivation and aligning tasks accordingly can maximize efficiency. This means tackling high-concentration assignments during natural energy peaks and reserving routine tasks for when we're feeling less focused. Such personalized scheduling aligns our work habits with our body's natural cycles, reducing stress and enhancing our overall output.

The challenge of managing stress inherent in a fast-paced digital environment isn't one to tackle alone. Encouraging a workplace culture that values wellness benefits not only individuals but also teams and organizations as a whole. Initiatives like mindfulness workshops or stress management programs can provide employees with the tools they need to thrive in demanding circumstances. Supporting each other in these efforts creates a collaborative atmosphere that reinforces both personal and professional development.

Ultimately, the pursuit of balancing productivity with wellbeing is a continuous journey. It's about creating a lifestyle where work is integrated into life in a harmonious way, rather than something that overshadows it. By valuing mindfulness as an essential component of our work ethic, we open ourselves to new ways of thinking and working that promote not just success but fulfillment and peace. This balance, though delicate, enables us to navigate the complexities of modern professional life with grace and resilience.

Chapter 18: Mindful Digital Learning

In an age where education is increasingly intertwined with technology, practicing mindfulness in digital learning offers a beacon of clarity amidst the vastness of online information. As tech-savvy individuals seek tranquility, embracing educational platforms mindfully becomes crucial. Imagine navigating through a sea of resources, yet returning with a clear sense of purpose and focus. It starts with setting intentional goals for each learning session, ensuring that digital engagements are empowering rather than overwhelming. Mindful digital learning isn't just about absorbing information—it's about engaging with content that resonates deeply. By fostering a disciplined approach with clear intentions, and routinely pausing to reflect, learners can transform digital tools into catalysts for genuine knowledge and growth. Techniques such as focused online learning harness the essence of presence, encouraging learners to cultivate attention amidst digital distractions. In this journey, mindfulness isn't merely an accessory; it's a pivotal ally that turns the chaos of constant connectivity into a structured path toward enlightenment.

Embracing Education Platforms

In our rapidly evolving digital age, education platforms have become an integral part of how we learn and grow. These platforms offer a tremendous potential to foster mindful learning practices that allow us to engage deeply with content while maintaining a balanced and serene digital life. The advancement of technology brings with it a chance to transform our educational experiences, allowing for a greater harmony between technology usage and mindfulness.

The beauty of education platforms lies in their flexibility and accessibility. They grant learners the ability to dictate their educational pace, opening up opportunities for self-reflection and awareness. When utilized mindfully, these platforms encourage a deeper understanding and appreciation of the learning journey. They allow for the integration of breaks and thoughtful pauses, giving time to assimilate information without overwhelming the senses. This flexibility empowers learners to tune into their motivations and energy levels, thus fostering a more conscious relationship with digital consumption.

Integrating mindfulness into education not only enriches the learning experience but also enhances cognitive focus and emotional well-being. By curating a space that promotes mindfulness, educators and learners can explore digital content with intention and purpose. This approach transforms learning from a mechanical transfer of information to a meditative process that involves the whole self. Taking a moment to breathe and reflect between learning modules can cultivate patience, attention, and a calm mind, thus enhancing overall engagement with the material.

For mindful learning to take root using digital platforms, it's essential to establish boundaries around digital engagement. This includes setting specific times for learning that align with one's peak cognitive hours and incorporating scheduled breaks to maintain mental acuity. Utilizing the built-in features of these platforms to manage notifications and limit distractions is another way to maintain focus and prevent burnout. By prioritizing these mindful practices, learners can create a digital environment that supports rather than detracts from their educational goals.

Moreover, the structured but adaptable nature of digital education platforms allows for the inclusion of diverse mindfulness techniques. These can range from short guided meditations to reflective journaling prompts that encourage students to connect deeply with the material. Instructors can weave mindfulness practices into curriculum design, creating a layered and holistic educational experience that addresses both the mind and the heart.

Mindful utilization of educational technology also involves critically assessing the tools and content available. It's about selecting platforms that resonate with one's learning style and providing content that is not only informative but also nurturing for the mind. This requires an awareness of the quality and sources of information, a skill that can be honed by engaging in mindfulness practices that enhance discernment and digital literacy. Such skills are invaluable in today's world, where information is abundant but not always beneficial.

The communal aspect of digital learning platforms can also be harnessed mindfully to foster a supportive learning environment. Discussion forums, virtual classrooms, and peer collaborations offer channels to share insights and experiences, contributing to a cumulative and conscious learning endeavor. Engaging mindfully in these communities promotes mutual respect, encourages empathy, and aids in building meaningful connections that enrich the learning process.

Ultimately, the mindful embrace of education platforms is about creating a balanced ecosystem where technology serves to augment, not dictate, the learning experience. As learners and educators explore these digital landscapes, maintaining an anchor in mindfulness ensures that the journey remains enriching and aligned with one's personal goals and values. It's a path that respects the wholeness of the individual and recognizes the profound interplay between inner contemplation and external knowledge.

As we continue to navigate the world of digital learning, the convergence of mindfulness and education technology becomes a beacon of sustainable growth and enlightened education practices. Through mindfulness, learners can transform their interactions with educational platforms, making learning a harmonious and life-affirming endeavor for today and the future.

Strategies for Focused Online Learning

In today's digital age, the allure of online learning is both undeniable and overwhelming. The convenience and accessibility of educational content are at an all-time high, yet so is the potential for distraction. It's no secret that focus is a prized commodity. How does one maintain attention amidst the relentless ping of notifications? This section delves into strategies designed specifically to enhance focus during online learning, offering approaches rooted in mindfulness to transform your educational journey.

Recognizing and controlling your environment is an essential first step. Begin by evaluating your learning space. Is it crowded with unnecessary tech or devices? If so, it's time to declutter. A minimalistic environment aids concentration and reduces mental clutter. Consider setting up a dedicated study area, distinct from spaces used for leisure or work. This physical separation helps signal the brain when to switch into learning mode, creating a mental boundary that optimizes focus.

Structuring your learning schedule is crucial. Unlike traditional classroom settings, online learning often lacks fixed schedules, making it easy to ignore time constraints. Committing to a consistent learning routine helps internalize discipline. Block specific times dedicated to study, ensuring frequent breaks to prevent burnout. These breaks, however brief, can rejuvenate the mind. A structured routine, when adhered to mindfully, fortifies concentration and maximizes learning outcomes.

Another powerful strategy lies in setting clear intentions before each session. Mindfulness begins with awareness, so start your session by identifying your objectives. Ask yourself what you intend to achieve. This clarity not only focuses your attention but also increases the likelihood of retaining information. It's about creating a mental roadmap, steering your learning journey with purpose and direction.

Pacing your learning is also vital. The human mind isn't programmed for marathon learning sessions without rest. Break your study material into manageable sections. Engage in what is often referred to as "chunking" — breaking down information into smaller, digestible units. This technique aids memory retention and minimizes overwhelming yourself with vast amounts of information at once.

Leveraging technology wisely can enhance learning rather than detract from it. Employ apps and tools designed to minimize distractions, such as website blockers or focus timers. These tools create a controlled digital environment that limits unnecessary digital interruptions, enabling a deeper engagement with the material. Mindfully selecting tech interventions can make a significant difference in how you absorb and interact with online content.

Remember that mindfulness in digital learning is not just about focusing but also about being present. Engage with your material actively. This isn't a passive absorption — it's a dynamic interaction. Ask questions, take notes, and participate in discussions if the platform allows. Engaging with the content on different levels not only improves understanding but reinforces the retention of concepts.

Regular reflection is another cornerstone strategy. Allocate time after each session to reflect on what you've learned. This intentional pause consolidates your understanding and can highlight areas needing more focus. Reflection is about both celebrating your progress and recognizing your challenges. It strengthens your learning path by making it adaptable and responsive to your needs.

Additionally, practicing self-compassion is vital. You're not a machine, and it's okay for your attention to falter sometimes. When it happens, gently redirect your focus back to the task at hand. Harsh self-criticism only adds to stress, whereas a kind awareness replenishes energy and motivation. Embrace learning as a journey, where mistakes are part of growth.

Utilizing social learning networks can add a layer of community and accountability. Platforms that offer peer interaction enhance motivation and engagement. Whether it's discussing topics, exchanging ideas, or supporting one another, social networks bring a sense of shared purpose and can invigorate your personal learning process.

Balance is also key. While it's easy to get engrossed, remember to balance online learning with offline activities. Physical movement, nature walks, and tactile hobbies offer breathing space for the mind. They rejuvenate mental faculties, making the time spent learning more effective. A balanced approach ensures sustainability in your educational efforts.

The journey of focused online learning, when anchored with mindfulness, offers more than knowledge acquisition. It transforms the process into a holistic experience where learning is not just about absorbing information but about cultivating awareness, intention, and presence. By adopting mindful strategies, you will not only learn more effectively but also appreciate the process, finding joy and fulfillment in your digital educational endeavors.

Chapter 19: Guiding Youth Towards Digital Mindfulness

In a world brimming with constant digital interactions, guiding the younger generation to develop mindfulness becomes essential. Encouraging youth to engage with technology mindfully can serve as a life skill, fostering balance and emotional well-being. It's not about eliminating technology but transforming how they perceive and interact with it. To help them thrive amidst digital distractions, parents, educators, and mentors must model mindful behaviors, teaching children to appreciate the moments of stillness and reflection amidst the digital rush. By incorporating simple practices like setting tech-free zones and having open conversations about online experiences, we can nurture an environment where young people learn to prioritize face-to-face interactions and embrace digital content with awareness. Equip them with the tools to understand and manage their digital consumption, and they will be better prepared to face technological advancements with clarity and intention.

Teaching Children to Navigate Technology

In today's hyper-connected world, teaching children to navigate technology with mindfulness is not just an option but a necessity. As screens become an integral part of their lives from an early age, parents and guardians face the challenge of guiding young minds towards a balanced digital existence. The key is to equip children with the tools they need to use technology responsibly, fostering a sense of curiosity and wonder without allowing it to dominate their lives.

One of the first steps in this journey is to encourage open conversations about technology. Engaging children in discussions about the digital tools they use can demystify technology and make it a shared family experience. This doesn't mean overseeing every online interaction, but rather fostering an environment where children feel comfortable sharing their digital experiences. Such dialog helps build trust and alleviates the pressure children might feel about hiding their online activities.

Parents can model mindful technology use by being conscious of their own habits. Children are highly observant and often emulate adult behavior. Therefore, putting away devices during family meals, designating tech-free times, and using technology visibly for positive purposes, such as learning new skills, can greatly influence a child's approach towards technology.

Establishing boundaries is another essential aspect of teaching mindful technology navigation. Setting clear rules about screen time, appropriate digital content, and online interactions provides children with a framework within which they can explore technology safely. These boundaries should be age-appropriate and flexible enough to adapt as children grow and technology evolves. Encouraging breaks away from screens to engage in physical activities or hobbies ensures that digital activity doesn't overshadow other vital areas of development.

Introducing children to the concept of digital mindfulness can be transformative. Mindfulness in digital contexts involves being present and aware while using technology. Teaching children to approach their devices with intention, such as asking themselves why they want to use a particular app or game, can lead them to more meaningful interactions. Incorporating mindfulness apps or engaging in short guided meditations before technology use can also help children cultivate a more centered digital presence.

Engagement with educational content online must be a priority over passive consumption. Encourage children to use technology as a tool for learning and creativity. Interactive apps, educational games, and online classes expand children's horizons and inspire them to think critically. These platforms provide controlled environments where children can safely explore various aspects of the digital world while stimulating their intellectual curiosity.

Another important aspect is teaching children about digital empathy. It's crucial to understand that behind every online interaction is a real person with feelings and experiences. Role-playing scenarios and discussing the potential impacts of cyberbullying or online gossip can sensitize children to the importance of being kind and respectful in their digital communications. These lessons in empathy will not only help them navigate technology mindfully but also create a safer online environment for their peers.

Parents should also foster resilience in children by preparing them for inevitable challenges that come with technology use. Kids must know that not everything they encounter online is positive or accurate. Critical thinking should be emphasized; children need the skills to discern reliable information from online noise. Encouraging them to question and verify digital content can empower them to make informed decisions.

Acknowledging and addressing digital fatigue is an often-overlooked aspect when teaching children about technology. Just like adults, children can experience exhaustion from prolonged screen use. Creating a family routine where digital downtime is encouraged helps children recognize the importance of unplugging. This practice not only rejuvenates their minds but also nurtures their ability to engage more profoundly with the digital world when they reconnect.

Technology is a powerful tool, but it is crucial to remind children of the world beyond screens. Weekend adventures, hands-on activities, and social interactions outside the digital realm enrich their experiences and provide a balanced perspective on life. These activities can also aid in developing a healthier relationship with technology by showing children the wonders of the physical world without digital mediation.

In conclusion, teaching children to navigate technology is about preparing them for a future that seamlessly blends digital and mindful experiences. As they grow up in an ever-evolving digital landscape, providing them with the right skills and ethical grounding ensures they're ready to handle whatever technological advancements come their way. This holistic approach to digital training can empower the next generation to harness the benefits of technology while maintaining the serenity and mindfulness that's essential for their well-being.

Developing Healthy Digital Habits

In the digital age, where screens permeate almost every aspect of our lives, fostering healthy digital habits becomes crucial, especially for the younger generation. Navigating this landscape with intention can be challenging, but not impossible. The key is to cultivate mindfulness in our interactions with technology, ensuring it serves as a tool for enrichment rather than a source of distress.

Developing these habits begins by understanding the impact that technology can have on our mental and physical well-being. For youth, who are particularly susceptible to the allure of digital platforms, having clear guidelines can serve as a compass. It's about making conscious choices that prioritize mental health and personal growth over incessant notifications and screen time.

To establish healthy digital habits, encourage the practice of setting regular breaks away from screens. This creates opportunities for reflection and self-awareness. Just as mindfulness encourages a pause and deep breath amidst life's chaos, stepping away from screens allows the brain to rest and reset. Implement this as a family routine, where time is dedicated to offline activities, fostering connections without digital interruptions.

One effective habit to instill is the practice of self-regulation. Teach young individuals to recognize their feelings as they engage with technology. Are they feeling stressed, overwhelmed, or anxious after time online? Encouraging checking in with oneself can prevent mindless scrolling and promote a more balanced interaction with digital content.

Another critical component is establishing a tech boundary. It's essential to define clear limits on technology use, such as designated times for checking social media or gaming. This isn't about imposing strict rules but about creating routines that offer freedom within boundaries. Encourage discussions around why these limits are beneficial, emphasizing the value of balance between the online and offline worlds.

Fostering an environment where youth can question and reflect on the content they consume online is also necessary. Empower them to think critically about what they read or watch, cultivating a discerning eye. This approach not only enhances digital literacy but also supports informed and conscious interactions with various platforms.

Promote the kind of technology use that sparks creativity rather than consumption. Encourage projects or activities where young people can use technology to create—whether it's digital art, movie-making, or coding. This shift from passive consumption to active creation nurtures a sense of accomplishment and purpose, transforming technology into a partner in creativity.

Sharing technology as a communal activity can also bridge digital divides within families. Engage in digital activities that involve collaboration and communication. Whether it's playing a game together, working on a digital project, or exploring a new app as a family, these shared experiences can diminish feelings of isolation and foster a supportive environment.

Mindful notifications are another strategy worth adopting. Encourage youth to curate their notification settings to minimize disturbances and ensure that their technology aligns with their priorities. This habit prioritizes focus and mental space over reacting to every ping and alert.

Incorporating mindfulness exercises into digital usage can also be beneficial. Whether it's taking a moment of stillness before starting an online session or practicing breathing techniques after logging off, these simple yet powerful practices can serve as anchors, bringing clarity and calm.

Furthermore, promoting a culture of gratitude in digital interactions can transform the online experience. Encouraging youth to acknowledge positive interactions and express gratitude digitally fosters a more supportive and uplifting digital environment.

Lastly, instilling the importance of variety within technology use helps prevent over-reliance on any single platform or device. Encourage exploring diverse content, platforms, and activities. This diversification can enrich experiences and prevent the pitfalls of monotony or addiction.

Ultimately, developing healthy digital habits for youth is about more than managing screen time; it's about equipping them with the skills and awareness to navigate digital landscapes mindfully and meaningfully. By embedding mindfulness into their digital lives, we're not just reducing potential harms; we're enhancing their ability to thrive in an increasingly connected world.

Our journey towards digital mindfulness, especially with the youth, requires patience, empathy, and dedication. It's about being aware of the evolving digital culture and continuously adapting strategies that nurture both technology's benefits and the well-being of young minds.

Chapter 20: Mindful Gaming

In the vibrant realm of gaming, mindfulness invites us to engage with intention and presence, transforming how we interact with digital landscapes. Instead of merely pursuing virtual victories, embracing mindful gaming means observing how play impacts our emotions and thoughts, fostering a deeper connection to ourselves and others. By setting clear boundaries and choosing games that align with our values, we create a gaming experience that nurtures rather than drains. This practice encourages us to view gaming not as an escape but as an opportunity for growth and reflection. Remember, mindful gaming is about savoring each moment, appreciating the artistry of the game, and being aware of how it fits into the broader tapestry of our lives. Let's approach this digital pastime with curiosity and awareness, uncovering insights that enhance our well-being both on and off the screen.

Approaching Video Games with Awareness

In a world where digital experiences flood our senses, video games hold a unique and nuanced position. For many of us, they're not just a way to pass time but a form of art, storytelling, and connection. But how do we engage with these virtual worlds mindfully? To start, it's essential to approach gaming with an intentional mindset, one that aligns with mindfulness. This involves understanding what we seek to gain from gaming and recognizing when it enhances or detracts from our well-being.

Mindful gaming means cultivating awareness about the content we're consuming and the emotional responses it evokes. At the heart of this practice is the question, "Why am I playing?" The answer isn't always straightforward; it might be to relax, to challenge ourselves, or to connect with friends. Whatever the reason, having clarity can transform how we perceive gaming. By setting this intention, we can distinguish between playing out of habit and playing for meaningful engagement.

Moreover, video games offer a mirror into our own psyche. They can reflect our problem-solving approaches, the patience we extend in tough situations, and even the stories that resonate with our personal narratives. Engaging with these insights can be profoundly enlightening. For instance, encountering repetitive patterns of frustration or joy can signal deeper themes in our lives, encouraging self-reflection and growth. Hence, treating video games as a potential tool for self-discovery brings a new dimension to our digital interactions.

Being mindful of the time spent on gaming is crucial too. It's easy to lose track, especially when we're deeply engrossed. Implementing structured time limits can help create balance. This doesn't mean cutting down enjoyment but ensuring that gameplay complements other life activities. Setting alarms or using gaming consoles' in-built timers can gently remind us to pause and carry out a quick reflection on how we're feeling in the moment.

Beyond time management, the choice of games plays a significant role in mindful gaming. Games come in various forms—some focus on strategy, others on story, and many on connections and competition. Selecting titles that align with our current needs or emotional states can profoundly affect our experience. If seeking relaxation, choose games with calm, exploratory elements. For those needing an intellectual challenge, strategy games might suit better. Aligning game choice with personal goals can turn gaming into a therapeutic activity rather than just entertainment.

In multiplayer gaming, maintaining awareness extends beyond personal experience into how we interact with others. Online platforms create opportunities for connection but also expose us to potential conflicts and stressors. Practicing empathy during these interactions, especially when emotions run high, can nurture a more positive and cooperative environment. Mindful communication strategies, learned from other areas of life, fit seamlessly into gaming, encouraging us to listen, understand, and often step back before responding.

Additionally, it's beneficial to periodically assess the emotional feedback loop created by gaming. Reflective journaling about in-game experiences can highlight recurring emotions or patterns that might otherwise go unnoticed. This is not to imply that every gaming session should lead to deep revelations, but awareness of emotional triggers prepares us for healthier engagement overall.

Video games, like any other digital medium, can also be integrated into collective mindfulness practices. Hosting gaming sessions with family or friends, where the intent is to share joy rather than just compete, adds a layer of mindfulness. Sharing perspectives on in-game experiences can be a gateway for meaningful conversations about life, goals, and emotional well-being.

Ultimately, just as mindfulness encourages living with intention, mindful gaming involves discerning how gaming fits into the broader tapestry of our lives. It means understanding both the escapism and engagement factors tied to our gaming habits. By doing so, we elevate gaming from a mere distraction to an activity that supports our pursuit of mindful living. This balance helps achieve harmony in our digital and real-world interactions, bridging a gap often considered vast and unbridgeable. Embracing video games with awareness ultimately contributes to our well-being, allowing us to enjoy the best of these digital landscapes while staying grounded in reality.

Positive Gaming Practices

Gaming often gets a bad rap when people talk about its potential to sap attention and lead to hours lost in virtual worlds. But it's possible to turn the gaming experience into a positive, mindful practice. Mindful gaming involves being fully present and aware of the choices you make within games, as well as the time you devote to playing them. With the right approach, you can transform gaming from a mindless activity into a beneficial and purposeful part of your digital toolkit.

One of the key aspects of positive gaming is setting clear intentions. Before you start playing, ask yourself why you're reaching for that controller or logging into your favorite online world. Are you seeking relaxation, connection with friends, or perhaps a bit of both? Having a clear intention can help you guide your gaming session in a way that aligns with your overall goals, preventing it from becoming a way to escape or avoid responsibilities.

Another important practice is to be aware of the time. It's easy to lose track when you're engrossed in a game, especially with designs that encourage prolonged engagement through rewards and achievements. Set a timer for yourself to keep gaming sessions from becoming open-ended marathons. Taking breaks not only helps maintain a healthy balance but also reduces the strain on your eyes and mind—ensuring that when you do dive back in, you're refreshed and ready to play with purpose.

Positive gaming also involves choosing games that foster creativity, strategic thinking, or cooperation. Many games are designed to stimulate the brain in beneficial ways, requiring players to think critically, make quick decisions, or work together to achieve a common goal. Furthermore, engaging with puzzle and strategy games can boost cognitive functions such as problem-solving and memory. It's about finding those games that not only entertain but also contribute to personal growth.

Developing a community can be another beneficial aspect of positive gaming. Many players find meaningful connections and friendships within online gaming communities. These digital spaces provide opportunities for shared experiences and can help foster a sense of belonging. By interacting with others who share your interests, you can add a social dimension to your gaming life, making it more than a solitary pastime.

At the same time, it's crucial to cultivate mindfulness in your interactions. Online anonymity can sometimes lead to negativity that detracts from positive gaming. Approach your gaming with empathy and understanding, recognizing that fellow players are real people with emotions and challenges of their own. Practicing kindness and patience, even in competitive environments, turns gaming into a platform for positive interactions.

Mindful gaming requires reflection. After a gaming session, take a moment to consider what you've learned and how you felt during the experience. Did the game leave you with a sense of satisfaction? Were there any moments of frustration, and how did you handle them? Reflecting on these aspects can offer insights into your own behaviors and help you adjust your gaming habits to enhance your well-being.

In incorporating positive gaming practices, being selective about the content you consume is equally vital. Just as you would choose nourishing food for your body, opt for games that contribute positively to your mental health. Avoid games that may trigger stress or promote negative emotions. Instead, aim for those that uplift your spirit or provide you with a sense of accomplishment.

It's also important to explore the creative outlets that gaming can offer. Many games today feature robust tools that allow players to create their own worlds or narratives. Engaging with these creative aspects can provide a way to express yourself and tap into your imaginative side, offering a unique form of relaxation and personal expression.

Finally, involve others in your gaming journey. Sharing this experience with friends or family can transform it into a bonding activity. Whether it's playing together or just discussing the games you love, involving your social circle in your gaming life can lead to enriched relationships and shared happiness.

Embracing positive gaming practices within your mindful lifestyle not only enhances your relationship with digital entertainment but also ensures that your gaming habits are in harmony with your mindful living goals. Gaming, when approached with intention and awareness, becomes a fulfilling endeavor rather than a distracting escape. As you integrate these practices, you'll find that gaming can contribute positively to your digital well-being, becoming a true extension of your mindful journey.

Chapter 21: Incorporating Mindful Breaks in Digital Routines

In a world where digital connectivity never sleeps, learning to carve out mindful breaks in your day can be transformative. Imagine your mind is a device that also requires periodic recharging. By consciously stepping away from screens, even for just a few moments, you can foster mental clarity and rejuvenate your energy levels. These pauses can't be haphazard; they need to be intentional. Consider, for instance, integrating simple practices like deep breathing exercises or brief moments of silent reflection. Such techniques act as quick resets, allowing you to return to your digital tasks with renewed focus and a sense of calm. This ongoing practice not only enhances productivity but also nurtures your well-being, crafting a harmonious balance between digital demands and personal tranquility. Let's explore how we can smoothly interlace these breaks into our daily routines, ensuring that our digital interactions contribute positively to our mental and emotional health.

Designing Breaks for Mental Clarity

In a world where every beep of our gadgets demands attention, finding moments of true stillness can seem impossible. Yet, incorporating mindful breaks into our digital routines is essential for maintaining mental clarity. Instead of viewing breaks as interruptions, we should perceive them as intentional pauses — opportunities to reset our minds and refresh our perspectives.

Consider the familiar feeling of digital fatigue. Eyes fixed on screens for hours, your mind becomes cluttered with unfinished tasks and infinite notifications. This constant barrage clouds your judgment and diminishes creativity. That's where thoughtfully designed breaks come into play. Far from halting productivity, these breaks refocus your energy, heightening efficiency and ensuring sustained performance.

Imagine a break as a mental palette cleanser. Just as artists reset their vision with a blank canvas, we can clear our minds through intentional pause. The key lies in how these breaks are orchestrated. Start with short pauses throughout the day — even a few minutes can suffice. Use this time to breathe deeply, stretch, or disconnect from screens.

Creating a mindful break environment is crucial. Designate a space in your surroundings as your "break zone". This space could be a cozy chair by a window or a spot in your garden. The location itself should evoke tranquility, encouraging you to step away from digital stressors.

During these breaks, resist the urge to pick up your phone. Instead, engage in simple mindfulness exercises. Focus on your breathing with eyes closed, or simply observe the world around you with a fresh perspective. Practicing mindfulness in these moments helps in realigning your thoughts and reconnecting with the present.

Consistent, structured breaks offer a powerful psychological benefit — the anticipation itself becomes a form of comfort, knowing relief is scheduled amid a packed schedule. This rhythm fosters a greater sense of control over your day and reduces the anxiety of feeling overwhelmed.

For tech enthusiasts and those deeply embedded in screen-heavy professions, technology itself can be harnessed constructively to create effective breaks. Utilize apps designed specifically for mindfulness to guide short meditation sessions or even breathing exercises. These tools, when used deliberately, act as allies rather than adversaries.

Balanced digital engagement requires understanding one's own limits. Personal experimentation can determine the optimal timing and duration of breaks. While some may rejuvenate with micro-breaks every hour, others might need longer pauses less frequently. Recognizing personal needs is part of harnessing the full potential of mindful breaks.

Furthermore, the principle of mindful breaks extends beyond individual practice. In a communal setting, peer groups or workplace teams can synchronize their break times. This collective pause fortifies relationships and encourages a culture of mindfulness, enabling mutual support in digital well-being.

While technology promises to amplify productivity, unchecked usage without engineered pauses can spiral into burnout. Mindful breaks are about rejuvenation and empowerment — reclaiming time previously lost to inefficient screen switching and scattered focus. Through them, we cultivate a grounded presence, which is crucial for clear decision-making.

Finally, remember that cultivating these breaks is an evolving practice. As life circumstances change, so too can the approach to these pauses. Flexibility and experimentation are part of discovering what revitalizes your unique system of focus.

Through intentional design of breaks for mental clarity, not only do we navigate the digital world more effectively, but we also nurture inner peace and focus. This mindful practice is less about detachment from technology and more about harmonious coexistence with it. Your digital life, when interspersed with mindful pauses, becomes not a source of distraction, but a part of a balanced, fulfilling existence.

Practices for Quick Resets

In the whirlwind of perpetual connectivity, finding a moment to breathe can feel like a luxury. However, a quick reset is not just a tool but a necessity for maintaining our mental well-being in a digital world. Unlike extended retreats or prolonged digital detoxes, quick resets are brief yet impactful practices that can be woven seamlessly into our daily routines. They allow us to regain our bearing, calm our minds, and restore our focus, even in the busiest of schedules.

Imagine this scenario: a notification pulls you out of your workflow. Suddenly, you're juggling tasks, emails, and messages. It happens to the best of us, and it's precisely in these moments that a quick reset can be invaluable. These brief breaks can range from one to five minutes, serving as a mental palate cleanser. The goal isn't to escape from work but to reset your mental state.

One simple yet powerful practice is the "breath check." It involves pausing to take several deep, conscious breaths. As you inhale, feel the cool air filling your lungs, and as you exhale, allow tension to seep away. This practice can be done seated, standing, or walking. It offers a moment to shift from autopilot to being fully present, enabling a calmer, more focused approach to subsequent tasks.

Beyond breath, the power of our senses can play a pivotal role in grounding us. The "5-4-3-2-1" technique leverages your senses to anchor you in the present. Start by acknowledging five things you can see, four you can touch, three you can hear, two you can smell, and one you can taste. This exercise isn't just about distraction; it's about shifting focus from digital interactions to the richness of the physical world around you.

A lesser-known yet effective reset method is called "micro-meditation." Find a comfortable position, close your eyes, and focus on a single thought or mantra for a minute or two. This practice can quiet the noise and recalibrate your mind, even amid digital chaos. For a minute, you let go of digital stimuli, which is often enough to return to your responsibilities with newfound clarity and intention.

Technology isn't the enemy; instead, it can be a companion in our quest for mindfulness. Mindfulness apps, though often associated with longer meditation sessions, offer quick reset features tailor-made for short breaks. Guided mini-sessions, lasting as short as two minutes, provide on-demand relief from digital stress. A few swipes on your smartphone transform it from a source of distraction into one of sanctuary.

Touch is another powerful ally in quick resets. You can engage with the digital world through physical sensations to break up screen time. A common practice is to have a stress ball or a piece of tactile art near your workspace. Pausing to manipulate it for a minute or so can shift your focus away from the digital screen and remind you of your physical environment. It's about reconnecting with the tangible world, providing a much-needed contrast to the scrolling and typing that dominates a tech-centric lifestyle.

Music and soundscapes also hold immense potential for quick resets. A dedicated playlist of calming or uplifting tunes can serve as your go-to for short breaks. Alternatively, nature sound apps or recordings—such as the soothing sound of waves, birdsong, or gentle rain—can swiftly transport you to a place of serenity. By creating a sound environment that contrasts the digital clamor, your brain can downshift and recharge efficiently.

For those working from home, stepping outside for a moment can be rejuvenating. Natural light and fresh air are often underrated energizers. Even a brief five-minute walk or standing in a patch of sunlight can lift your mood and help recalibrate your focus. Nature doesn't just influence the mind positively; it nourishes the soul, even when appreciated in microdoses.

Additionally, movement, however modest, can work wonders. A few yoga stretches or even a bit of conscious movement at your desk can invigorate your body. It doesn't have to be elaborate—something as simple as standing up and stretching can break the monotony of sitting and screen-gazing. These small practices remind us that we're not bound to our desks and screens, despite the demands on our time.

When exploring practices for a quick reset, remember there's no one-size-fits-all solution. Each person has unique triggers and preferences, so it's about experimenting with different techniques to find what resonates best with you. It might be a combination of several methods—like spending 30 seconds on a breath check followed by a minute of nature sounds—which offers the best results.

Above all, approach these practices with a sense of curiosity and compassion. Quick resets are not just about efficiency; they're about kindness toward yourself in digital chaos. View them as gentle pauses that validate your need for mental space and rejuvenation. Even in a hyper-connected world, moments to reset are accessible and vital to our nuanced life.

In practicing these quick resets, we embrace a future where digital life is not a burden but a mindful journey. We grant ourselves permission to step back, breathe, and realign, ultimately fostering a balanced relationship with technology that's both intentional and enriching. As we continue exploring this journey, remember the words of old wisdom—that sometimes, the fastest route lies in the blessed pause.

Chapter 22: Environmental Impact of Technology

As we continue our journey towards finding tranquility amidst the digital onslaught, it's crucial to pause and reflect on the environmental footprint of our technological habits. Each swipe, click, and stream defines not just our personal routines but contributes to a larger, often invisible, ecological impact. The convenience of cloud storage, the allure of streaming services, and the never-ending cycle of device upgrades all demand energy and resources. Becoming mindful of our digital consumption doesn't mean abandoning technology but embracing more sustainable practices. Simple changes, like reducing unnecessary data usage or thoughtfully selecting energy-efficient devices, can lead to a collective positive impact on our planet. This awareness not only fosters a healthier environment but also aligns with our quest for a mindful digital life—encouraging us to live and interact with intention. Each conscious choice you make is a step toward harmonizing technology with the natural world, creating a balance that honors both our planet and our peace of mind.

Understanding Digital Footprint

Picture the swirls of energy and resources akin to the ripples in a pond, each one representing a piece of our digital interactions. All of these, from the simplest web search to massive data centers, culminate in what we term as the "Digital Footprint". This concept refers to the trail of data we leave behind through our online activities, intentionally or otherwise. It's a reflection of our digital lives' environmental impact—a subject often overshadowed by the convenience of technology.

Every click, every email, every streamed video contributes to this footprint. As technology-savvy individuals, we're often focused on the benefits of technological advances while overlooking their environmental repercussions. Yet, technology-driven activities consume immense amounts of energy, contributing significantly to carbon emissions. The seemingly infinite cloud, for instance, is powered by real-world data centers that use substantial electricity often generated from non-renewable sources. Understanding this helps anchor our choices in the reality that digital convenience isn't environmentally neutral.

Our responsibility, then, is to bring mindfulness to how we use technology. Consider how server farms operate relentlessly, generating heat that requires extensive cooling solutions. This illustrates how our digital actions have far-reaching environmental consequences. A seemingly innocuous online purchase triggers a cascade involving databases, processing, and delivery logistics, each adding to the cumulative carbon footprint.

So, how do we align our tech habits with mindful living? First, we must acknowledge the invisible energy footprint behind our routines. Sprawling data centers, while essential, account for a larger greenhouse gas emission share than the aviation industry. A typical HD video streaming binge, for example, means far more than leisurely viewing; it translates into increased data transmission and energy use.

Developing awareness is essential. Start by questioning the necessity of every digital interaction. Is it essential, or are we merely acting on autopilot? By cultivating this introspection, we naturally begin to refine our choices, reducing unnecessary interactions and savoring those we choose to keep. The practice of deliberate decision-making isn't just healthy for our psyche; it's a step toward sustainability.

You don't have to sacrifice connectivity for consciousness. Instead, look towards optimizing your digital practices. Take cloud storage: by selectively storing files offline or cleaning out digital clutter, you reduce the load and energy demands on remote servers. Additionally, opting for renewable-powered service providers can make a tangible difference. Evaluate your browsers for energy-efficient alternatives and favor those with resource-saving features. It's about mindful consumption, not deprivation.

Furthermore, supporting innovation is vital. Encouraging tech companies that aim for sustainability is another step towards reducing the digital footprint. Many companies are now striving to blend technological advancement with environmental responsibility. Investing time in researching these options ensures that your digital choices foster an industry moving towards greener standards.

Consider, too, the lifespan of our devices. From production to disposal, every gadget tells its own ecological story packed with resource extraction, factory emissions, and eventual e-waste challenges. Prioritizing durability over the latest upgrade, and recycling devices responsibly, should form part of our mindful tech habits. Repair instead of replace when feasible, and explore options to repurpose technology creatively within your community.

In conclusion, understanding the digital footprint is more than counting bytes; it's an awakening to the environmental impact of our digital existence. Through mindful engagement, we're not just passive users but active stewards of both our digital and natural worlds. By marrying technological innovation with eco-conscious scrutiny, we lay the groundwork for a sustainable digital future that inspires both serenity and responsibility in our tech-savvy lives. The path to harmony lies in awareness, and the journey begins with each informed choice we make.

Mindful Consumption of Technology

As our lives integrate seamlessly with the digital realm, the environmental impacts of technology cannot be ignored. The devices we use daily, the data centers powering the cloud, and even the apps that keep us connected all require energy and resources, often at the expense of the planet. But mindful consumption of technology offers us a way to harmonize our digital habits with ecological responsibility.

Mindfulness in the context of technology encourages us to pause and reflect on our consumption patterns. It's about recognizing our individual digital footprint and the collective impact it contributes to environmental degradation. This awareness isn't merely about using less; it's about using more thoughtfully.

Consider the energy consumption of data centers. These facilities, essential for cloud computing, are significant sources of carbon emissions. By curbing excessive data usage and unnecessary digital storage, we contribute to a reduction in energy consumption. Practicing digital minimalism can be a potent strategy in this regard. By decluttering our devices and reducing redundant files and apps, we reduce the demand for additional storage and processing power, which in turn decreases our ecological footprint.

Similarly, every time we upgrade to the latest device, we're contributing to electronic waste, a growing environmental concern. Mindful tech consumption might mean extending the life of our current devices. Repair rather than replace, consider second-hand options, and recycle responsibly. Making conscious choices about when and what to upgrade can significantly impact the environment.

Moreover, the platforms and services we choose matter. Opt for those that prioritize sustainability. Interestingly, many tech companies are now striving for energy efficiency and carbon neutrality. Supporting these companies can drive industry-wide environmental change.

There is also a mindfulness practice in optimizing the way we use technology during our routines. Lower the brightness of your screens, use energy-saving settings, and switch off devices when not in use. These small changes, collectively and consistently applied, can save a remarkable amount of energy.

Yet, mindful technology consumption transcends the physical realm. It involves consciously choosing which information to consume, thus reducing the digital noise contributing to mental and environmental clutter. Streamline your digital life; subscribe only to necessary channels and services, curate the notifications you receive, and control the flow of information.

This approach not only benefits the environment but also enhances personal well-being. A digital life less cluttered is one with room for tranquility and focus. It allows us to engage more deeply with the content we cherish, instead of being overwhelmed by an avalanche of digital detritus.

The goal, ultimately, is to align our tech usage with our values. By consuming technology mindfully, we contribute to a sustainable future, one where technology and the environment don't oppose each other but coexist in balance.

Incorporating mindfulness into our technology practices isn't just about reducing consumption; it's about redefining connection. By pursuing intentional interactions with our devices, we can foster a deeper connection to the world around us—a world in which our digital and natural lives support and sustain one another.

Remember, every choice counts. The shift towards more sustainable technology habits starts with individual actions but has the potential for profound global impact. By leading by example, we can inspire others to consider the broader implications of their digital lives. Our mindful choices today lay the groundwork for a technologically advanced but environmentally conscious tomorrow.

Finally, let's remind ourselves that technology is a tool—how we utilize it shapes it for good or ill. By embracing the practices of mindful consumption, we ensure that we not only enjoy the benefits of innovation but also act as guardians of our planet.

Chapter 23: Privacy and Digital Peace

In an era where our lives are increasingly interwoven with technology, maintaining a sense of privacy is not just about safeguarding data, but also about nurturing one's mental tranquility. Embracing mindfulness in the digital space requires a balanced approach, ensuring that while technology keeps evolving, our personal space remains sacred. It's about being intentional with the information we share and setting boundaries that protect our peace. By cultivating awareness of our online behavior—what we disclose, how we interact, and where our data travels—we build a sanctuary amidst the digital chaos. This practice does more than secure information; it fosters a profound sense of peace, allowing us to engage with technology in a way that supports rather than disrupts our mindful journey. Our digital lives become not a source of stress but a landscape where clarity and calm flourish, leading us towards a harmonious coexistence with the technology that surrounds us.

Protecting Personal Information

In our quest for digital peace, protecting personal information stands as a cornerstone. It's essential to strike a balance between the convenience technology offers and the privacy we need for mental tranquility. The journey to maintaining privacy starts with awareness, acknowledging that every click, like, or share leaves an indelible mark on our digital landscape.

We live in an era where personal data flows seamlessly across borders, becoming the new currency in the digital age. It's no longer just about guarding social security numbers or bank details. Today, personal data includes everything from browsing habits to location history. This vast array of information can paint an intimate portrait of our lives, and in the wrong hands, it can feel like an invasion. The first step toward digital privacy, therefore, is understanding what information you're willingly—or unwittingly—sharing.

To begin, cultivate a mindful approach to your digital existence. This starts with reflecting on what you're comfortable sharing and why. Consider each piece of information not just in terms of necessity but also in terms of its potential implications. Are you aware of how your data could be repurposed or who might gain access to it? Asking these questions can be the difference between uninhibited sharing and thoughtful discretion.

Empower yourself by learning the nuances of privacy settings. Many platforms offer granular controls over what data is collected and how it's used. Delve into these settings and tailor them to match your comfort level. Such adjustments might seem trivial, but they're vital steps in safeguarding your digital footprint. Don't underestimate the power of small changes; they collectively weave a robust shield around your personal information.

Befriend two-factor authentication (2FA). Though it might seem like an extra step, 2FA adds a formidable layer of defense. By requiring not just a password but also a second form of verification, such as a text message or authentication app, you significantly bolster your account's security. It's about making your digital doors just a little harder for unwanted guests to breach. And remember, strong passwords are your first line of defense. Length and randomness make them difficult to crack, so don't skimp on their complexity.

Another protective measure is being mindful of your online presence. Adoption of a less-is-more philosophy online can be liberating. Consider reducing the number of platforms where your information is shared. Audit your digital footprint regularly by reviewing old accounts or apps you no longer use, and take the time to delete what's obsolete. Each inactive account is a potential vulnerability waiting to be exploited.

Phishing attempts and malware are ever-present threats in our interconnected world. Developing a keen sense of skepticism can save you from countless digital dangers. Be cautious of unsolicited messages and unexpected links or attachments. Verify the source before engaging with anything that seems even slightly off. Trust your instincts—if something doesn't feel right, it probably isn't.

While technology companies often promise data protection, it's important to remember that their primary goal is often different from our personal privacy needs. Thus, being proactive is key. Utilize tools like virtual private networks (VPNs) to encrypt your internet connection, hiding your IP address and making your browsing activities more private. These tools are not just for tech enthusiasts; they're accessible to anyone wishing to add an extra veil of protection.

Additionally, consider the data implications of the apps and services you use daily. Some applications come with a hefty price: free services that cost you your data. Before downloading, take a moment to review privacy policies and terms of service. Understand what you're agreeing to. These long documents can seem daunting, but even a skim to catch crucial points regarding data usage and sharing can be revealing.

Moreover, think twice before sharing personal information with seemingly trustworthy services. Even beloved platforms can face breaches, leaving your data exposed. Take steps such as using pseudonyms or alternate email addresses to add layers of separation between your true identity and your online activities.

With the rise of the Internet of Things (IoT), our personal data extends beyond the virtual world into our physical environments. Smart devices, from watches to refrigerators, collect data with every interaction. It's crucial to recognize that privacy extends into these new realms. Adjust settings on these devices, turn off unnecessary data sharing, and regularly update software to patch vulnerabilities.

Practice a culture of transparency with family and friends. Share techniques you've found effective, and create a dialogue about respecting each other's privacy. Encouraging digital literacy within your circle strengthens everyone's protective measures and builds a community informed about maintaining personal information security.

Ultimately, protecting personal information is an ongoing process that requires vigilance and adaptability. It's not about shutting ourselves off from technology but rather navigating it with awareness and control. By prioritizing privacy, we not only protect our personal interests but also cultivate a deeper sense of digital peace, creating a harmonious balance in our tech-driven lives.

Staying Safe and Mindful Online

In today's hyper-connected world, maintaining one's online safety while practicing mindfulness can feel like a daunting task. However, finding a balance between protecting personal information and maintaining a sense of calm is essential for those seeking digital peace. The rapid expansion of digital interactions demands that we not only guard our privacy but also do so with intention and awareness.

One of the fundamental steps toward safety online starts with a shift in perspective about our digital interactions. Instead of viewing security measures as burdens, think of them as tools for preserving peace. Just as we lock the front door to safeguard our physical space, adopting a mindful approach to online security is about feeling secure enough to focus on what truly matters. This mindset helps reduce anxiety associated with potential digital threats.

Begin by regularly auditing your digital footprints. Knowing where your data resides is empowering. Regularly updating passwords, using two-factor authentication, and staying informed about privacy settings on profiles and devices are some practices that can be seamlessly integrated into a mindful digital routine. Consider them as acts of self-care rather than just chores.

An often overlooked aspect of maintaining safety online is cultivating digital discernment. In the age of information overload, it's crucial to evaluate the intentions behind the content we engage with or share. Each piece of information we interact with can impact our mental state. Ask yourself: Does this add value? Is it from a credible source? Pausing before following a sensation-driven headline or viral trend can preserve one's peace of mind.

Mindful interaction extends to the sphere of social media as well. These platforms, while connecting us with friends and communities, are often breeding grounds for stress and misinformation. Practicing mindful engagement here means curating your feed to reflect positivity, utility, and inspiration. Employ strategies like digital detoxes or setting boundaries for social media use, which are discussed further in other chapters, to mitigate the risks and cultivate a serene online experience.

The essence of mindfulness is awareness and conscious choice. Applying this to technology involves deliberate action—not just automatically tapping or scrolling. This can turn potential threats into opportunities for growth and connection. Cultivate a habit of periodically reviewing app permissions and understanding the data collection policies of the services you use. It enables you to engage mindfully, ensuring that you are comfortable with the level of personal information you're sharing.

In maintaining online privacy, it's not merely about what we do but how we do it. For instance, some may find solace in establishing digital havens—personal spaces online where they can reflect without interruption. This could be a blog, a personal journal app, or even a community forum filled with like-minded individuals. These spaces become sanctuaries for mindful reflection and self-expression without the distraction of constant notifications or persuasion of ads.

Another powerful practice is setting intentions before entering online spaces. With each login, ask yourself: What is my purpose in this digital moment? Be it checking emails, participating in social media discussions, or reading news updates, approaching these tasks with a clear goal can minimize mindless interaction and maximize fulfilment.

Moreover, fostering a sense of control over your digital environment contributes significantly to preserving digital peace. Customize notifications to alert you only when necessary or designate specific times of the day for checking updates. In doing so, you create a buffer against the bombardment of information and reclaim your focus.

Cultivating an understanding of common online hazards—scams, phishing attempts, and malicious software—fortifies our ability to navigate the web safely. Simple mindfulness exercises, like taking a deep breath before clicking on a suspicious link or responding to a questionable email, can prevent hasty decisions and reduce risk.

The journey toward staying safe and mindful online is ongoing but rewarding. By weaving these principles into our daily digital engagements, we invite a sense of harmony that resonates far beyond the screen. As we build these habits, we'll find that achieving digital peace isn't about isolation, but rather about intention and connection in our online worlds.

Embracing this mindful approach to online safety does more than protect us; it enhances the quality of our interactions and enriches our relationship with technology. Through the dual lens of security and mindfulness, we craft a digital experience that supports our well-being, fosters authentic connections, and ultimately contributes to a harmonious life, seamlessly integrating with our mindful practices offline.

Chapter 24: Mindful Leadership in the Digital Age

In today's fast-paced digital world, leadership demands a renewed focus on mindfulness to cultivate environments where both technology and humanity can flourish. As leaders, we face the challenge of guiding teams through a ceaseless tide of information and constant connectivity. To lead mindfully means embodying presence, fostering open and empathetic communication, and setting an example of balance in digital consumption. It's about finding that sweet spot where technological innovation meets human intuition, encouraging teams to disconnect when necessary to recharge and gain clarity. Mindful leadership invites a deeper awareness, not just of the digital tools we utilize every day, but of the people and feelings we navigate through this interconnected existence. By developing conscious leadership qualities, we foster spaces where creativity thrives, and stress diminishes, ultimately steering our digital age towards a future where productivity and well-being coexist harmoniously.

Developing Conscious Leadership Qualities

In the digital age, the concept of leadership has evolved to require more than just strategic thinking and decision-making. Conscious leadership is about being fully present, empathetic, and aware of the broader impact of one's actions—not only in the physical world but also in the digital sphere. As technology becomes more integrated into our daily lives, leaders are challenged to navigate their responsibilities consciously, ensuring harmony between technological advancements and human values.

Conscious leadership begins with self-awareness. Leaders must first understand their thoughts, emotions, and biases. This is not a one-time task but an ongoing process of introspection. Modern leaders often find themselves amidst a flurry of digital notifications, emails, and virtual meetings that demand constant attention. They must recognize the impact of this perpetual digital noise on their state of mind and decision-making abilities. Developing consciousness in such an environment requires intentional pauses to reset and recenter oneself. Take small moments throughout the day to disconnect and reconnect with your inner self, allowing for reflective thought.

A fundamental quality of conscious leaders is empathy. In the context of the digital age, this means striving to understand the experiences and challenges of team members who may be working remotely or in different time zones. Virtual communication often lacks the nuances of face-to-face interaction, making it crucial for leaders to go beyond words, listening deeply to understand underlying emotions and intentions. This is where mindful communication, covered in detail elsewhere in this book, becomes essential. By cultivating empathy, leaders not only enhance their own awareness but also foster a supportive and inclusive work environment.

Moreover, conscious leaders in the digital realm must navigate the ethical implications of technology use. With AI and big data becoming integral to business processes, understanding the ethical ramifications of these tools is vital. Leaders need to be proactive in promoting ethical practices and ensuring transparency in how data is used within their organizations. This kind of informed decision-making extends beyond business results; it's about considering the long-term societal impacts and making choices that align with ethical and moral values.

One key aspect of developing conscious leadership is fostering a culture of mindfulness within the workplace. Leaders can set the tone by modeling mindfulness practices, such as mindful meetings, where deliberate attention and presence are emphasized. Encourage teams to participate in mindfulness workshops or incorporate short mindfulness exercises into the workday. By promoting a culture of presence, organizations can benefit from increased focus, creativity, and collaboration, while individuals experience reduced stress and burnout.

In addition to cultivating personal mindfulness, conscious leaders actively seek to balance productivity with well-being. The relentless pace of digital communication often leads to blurred lines between work and personal life. Leaders must be vigilant in creating and respecting boundaries, advocating for work-life balance within their teams. They should champion policies that support digital rest, allowing team members to recharge and remain mentally healthy and productive in the long term.

Conscious leaders also embrace change with a mindful mindset. The digital landscape is constantly shifting, with new technologies and trends emerging at an unprecedented pace. Being open to adaptation while staying anchored in core values is essential. This involves staying informed, critically evaluating new tools, and integrating those that align with the organization's mission and ethical standards. Remaining adaptable, yet discerning, allows leaders to steer their teams through technological evolution without losing sight of human-centric goals.

Another profound aspect of conscious leadership lies in understanding one's influence and using it responsibly. In a hyper-connected world, every action taken in the digital domain has the potential for vast ripple effects. Leaders must be mindful of the narratives they endorse, the behaviors they model, and the platforms they choose to engage with. Conscious leadership entails leveraging digital influence to inspire positive change, fostering an environment where technology serves humanity rather than dominates it.

Furthermore, as leadership in the digital age involves guiding diverse teams often spread across different geographical locations, cultural mindfulness becomes crucial. Leaders should cultivate an awareness of diverse cultural backgrounds and practices, embracing diversity as a strength. This requires sensitivity to various communication styles and the willingness to learn from diverse perspectives, enhancing the collective intelligence and innovation within the team.

The journey toward conscious leadership in the digital age is not a solitary endeavor. It requires the support and collaboration of peers, mentors, and team members. Encouraging open dialogue about mindfulness and its integration into daily work practices fosters a collective effort toward achieving conscious leadership goals. This shared pursuit not only strengthens individual leaders but also builds a community of mindful practitioners who support and hold each other accountable.

Ultimately, developing conscious leadership qualities is a holistic process that encompasses personal reflection, empathetic engagement, ethical stewardship, and mindful collaboration. By embracing these principles, leaders can navigate the complexities of the digital world with wisdom and grace, forging a path that prioritizes human connection and well-being in an age of relentless technological progress.

Techniques for Leading with Presence

In the fast-paced digital age, effective leadership is not just about making the right decisions; it's about embodying a presence that inspires and connects people. The constant barrage of notifications, emails, and digital demands can easily pull a leader in multiple directions, leaving them feeling fragmented and stressed. Mindful leadership offers a pathway through this chaos, providing techniques that encourage leaders to ground themselves amidst the noise. By leading with presence, leaders can cultivate a more mindful and intentional workplace, ultimately driving both personal and organizational success.

One foundational technique for leading with presence in the digital age is the practice of deep listening. In a world where surface-level conversations are often the norm due to time constraints and the brevity of digital communication, deep listening requires a conscious effort. It involves engaging with others in a way that is fully attentive, setting aside devices, distractions, and preconceptions. When leaders listen deeply, they hear the words being spoken and capture the unspoken emotions and intentions behind them. This fosters trust and encourages openness, which are crucial elements of effective leadership.

Setting clear intentions before engaging in any interaction is another valuable technique. When leaders take a moment to define what they hope to achieve from a meeting or a conversation, they enter the interaction with clarity and purpose. This intention-setting can be as simple as pausing for a breath before a virtual meeting to remind oneself of the goal, whether it's to reach a decision, solve a problem, or simply connect with a team member. By anchoring interactions with intention, leaders can navigate digital communications with a focused and mindful approach.

Mindful leadership also extends into the realm of emotional awareness. Leaders who are attuned to their own emotions can better manage their responses to the challenges and stresses of digital interactions. Techniques such as mindfulness meditation and body scans help leaders remain attuned to their emotional states, recognizing when they are feeling stressed, frustrated, or overwhelmed. By acknowledging these feelings without judgment, leaders can respond with greater wisdom and calmness. This emotional regulation not only benefits the leaders themselves but also sets a tone of emotional stability within the team.

Practicing presence in leadership is incomplete without understanding and leveraging the power of pauses. In an era characterized by hasty replies and instant messaging, the art of pausing may seem counterintuitive. However, incorporating pauses into conversations or decision-making processes allows for deeper reflection and enhanced mindfulness. A moment's pause can provide clarity, enabling leaders to choose their words deliberately and make decisions that align with their values and the organization's goals.

Additionally, fostering a culture of mindfulness within teams can amplify a leader's presence. Encouraging team members to engage in mindful practices, such as short meditation sessions or mindfulness-based stress reduction exercises, can create a shared environment that values presence. By modeling mindfulness and creating space for these practices, leaders set the stage for a team that collectively values attention, clarity, and well-being. Such a culture not only enhances productivity but also contributes to a supportive and cohesive team dynamic.

Leaders can also adopt the technique of mindful delegation to enhance their presence and efficiency. In the digital age, understanding when to delegate and when to take action personally is crucial. Mindful delegation involves making strategic choices about task assignments, based on an understanding of team members' strengths, workloads, and development needs. By entrusting responsibilities mindfully, leaders empower their teams while freeing themselves to focus on strategic and high-priority matters that require their unique insights and presence.

Creating digital boundaries is another crucial technique for leading with presence. This involves establishing clear guidelines on when and how to engage with digital tools and platforms. Leaders who actively manage their connectivity—designating specific times for checking emails or setting aside no-tech zones—demonstrate a commitment to balance and focus. This conscious management of digital interactions allows leaders to be fully present in their offline engagements, be it with team members, partners, or during personal moments.

Furthermore, embracing authenticity in digital communication is a key technique for maintaining presence. In digital interactions where nonverbal cues are limited, authenticity can seem diminished. Yet, by being genuine and transparent in their communications, leaders can enhance their presence. This might involve sharing successes and challenges openly, admitting when they don't have all the answers, and actively soliciting inputs from team members. Such authenticity resonates with teams, fuels engagement, and strengthens the leader's presence.

For leaders, personal well-being practices are indispensable in sustaining presence. Techniques such as maintaining a routine of physical exercise, mindful nutrition, and sufficient rest play an integral role in equipping leaders with the energy and focus needed to maintain presence. Such practices not only benefit the individual leader but also ripple through the organization, promoting a culture where well-being is prioritized alongside performance.

In summary, leading with presence in the digital age involves a tapestry of techniques that integrate mindfulness into every aspect of leadership. From listening deeply and setting clear intentions to cultivating emotional awareness and fostering mindful cultures, these practices empower leaders to navigate complexities with authenticity and intentionality.

By incorporating mindful delegation, digital boundaries, and personal well-being, leaders can sustain their presence and drive both personal and organizational growth in today's fast-evolving digital landscape.

Chapter 25: The Future of Digital Mindfulness

The fast-paced evolution of technology doesn't mean we must relinquish tranquility and awareness to a sea of endless notifications and demands. Instead, this era invites us to redefine our relationship with digital spaces by thoughtfully integrating mindfulness practices into our connected lives. As emerging trends suggest a more immersive and constant connectivity, the key lies in cultivating an adaptable mindfulness, one that evolves alongside technological advancements. The future holds promise with innovative tools designed to foster presence and intention, weaving these qualities seamlessly into our daily digital interactions. By embracing a mindful approach, we not only enhance our personal well-being but also contribute to a more compassionate and focused digital community. Let's prepare for the future by anchoring ourselves in the present, ensuring that emerging technologies serve as allies in our journey towards conscious living.

Emerging Trends and Insights

In today's ever-evolving digital landscape, the intersection of mindfulness and technology is becoming increasingly nuanced, offering both challenges and opportunities. As we consider the future of digital mindfulness, emerging trends point toward an integrated approach that leverages innovation while anchoring us in presence and intentionality. One can't ignore the rapid pace of technological advancement—constantly offering novel ways to interact, engage, and sometimes, overwhelm. However, these shifts also bring fresh opportunities for fostering a more mindful digital existence.

Technological companies are beginning to recognize the demand for digital wellness features, integrating mindfulness into the very tools we use daily. Smartphones now come with built-in screen time trackers and focus modes designed to reduce unnecessary digital distractions. It's an acknowledgment of our need to balance tech use with well-being. This shift isn't just about limiting our digital engagement; it encourages intentional use where every notification, app, or device interaction adds meaningful value to our lives.

Moreover, businesses are starting to incorporate mindfulness into their ethos, promoting not just products, but digital experiences that foster well-being. The emphasis is on creating user experiences that enhance rather than detract from quality of life. For example, social media platforms are experimenting with features that limit exposure to harmful content and encourage conscious interaction. While these changes reflect a growing awareness of the need for digital mindfulness, they also illustrate a foundational shift in how companies perceive their role in users' lives.

Emerging data suggest that as more users become conscious of their digital habits, there's a growing movement toward digital minimalism. This approach isn't about rejecting technology but rather curating it; focusing on what truly matters and jettisoning the digital excess. People are increasingly asking themselves what technologies genuinely enhance their lives, and are making deliberate choices accordingly. Whether it's selecting apps that promote well-being or embracing digital tools that offer clarity, this trend reflects a broader desire to harmonize one's digital presence with a mindful lifestyle.

AI and machine learning also play pivotal roles in the future of digital mindfulness. Emerging AI tools are being designed not just to increase efficiency, but to enhance focus and promote mindfulness. Imagine AI-driven assistants that help you choose when to disconnect, suggesting activities that encourage mental clarity and well-being. Such tools can potentially act as guardians of our attention, not merely demanding it. These advancements necessitate a careful balancing act, ensuring AI aids rather than distracts.

Virtual reality (VR) and augmented reality (AR) offer another frontier in mindful digital interaction. As these technologies advance, their potential to create immersive mindfulness experiences grows exponentially. Imagine donning a VR headset and finding yourself in a serene Japanese garden, practicing mindfulness meditation with personal guidance from a virtual instructor. Such applications could revolutionize how we engage with mindfulness practices, making them accessible to anyone, anywhere, at any time. The potential here is immense, yet it requires a judicious approach to ensure these virtual experiences promote genuine peace rather than superficial distraction.

In parallel, the growing trend of 'digital detox' retreats highlights society's increasing recognition of the need to unplug. These retreats, often held in nature-rich environments, combine traditional mindfulness techniques with moderated tech usage. They cater to an audience yearning for solace from the constant digital barrage, offering structured environments to rediscover balance and tranquility. This movement signals a broader cultural shift toward valuing time away from screens as essential to mental well-being.

The future of digital mindfulness also encompasses education, both formal and informal. Educational institutions and online platforms are recognizing their role in fostering mindful tech use from an early age. There's a burgeoning development of curricula aimed at teaching children digital mindfulness, positioning tech as a tool for creativity, learning, and connection rather than a source of distraction or stress. These initiatives are crucial, educating the next generation on how to engage with digital spaces mindfully and instilling habits that promote lifelong digital well-being.

While the intersection of mindfulness and technology offers exciting possibilities, it also presents challenges that require careful navigation. The increased dependency on digital solutions calls for ongoing education about privacy, security, and ethical tech use. As more data is collected and algorithms become more sophisticated, maintaining digital peace and personal autonomy is increasingly complex. Mindfulness practices must evolve to help individuals maintain a sense of security and control over their digital narrative.

Finally, the role of community in digital mindfulness cannot be overstated. As trends move toward more communal tech experiences—think online meditation groups or digital mindfulness challenges—there is an opportunity to build supportive networks that encourage collective growth. These communities can become incubators for sharing best practices and providing mutual support, fostering a culture of mindful engagement that transcends individual efforts.

As we venture forward, digital mindfulness must continually adapt to the shifting tech landscape. It's not a static goal but an evolving journey requiring attentiveness, flexibility, and innovation. By embracing these emerging trends and insights, we can harness technology to enhance mindfulness, ensuring a more balanced, intentional digital future for all.

Preparing for Continuous Connection

We're living in an era where digital connectivity is increasingly becoming indispensable. The threads of our daily routines are woven tightly with technology, from the moment we wake up to the time we go to bed. This reality poses a unique challenge: How do we prepare for continuous connection while maintaining a sense of mindfulness and balance? To tackle this, one has to adopt practices that not only embrace technology but create a buffer of tranquility amidst its incessant chatter.

The first step lies in acknowledging that our digital devices don't just demand our attention—they thrive on it. Notifications, updates, and constant pings can overwhelm even the most disciplined minds. What if we could transform our relationship with these prompts? Mindfulness invites us to shift from a reactive state to a proactive stance. This means crafting our digital environments to serve us rather than enslave us. Consider scheduling specific times for checking emails or messages rather than reacting instantly. This practice fosters a sense of control and reduces anxiety caused by the need to always be "on."

Building digital rituals can serve as anchor points that center us. For instance, beginning the day with a few moments of mindful breathing before reaching for the smartphone can set a tone of intentionality. It's about creating a digital frame that supports rather than disrupts your inner peace. This might involve using tech tools mindfully—for example, employing apps that promote meditation or focus—rather than those that simply occupy time.

In this digital age, silence is a rare commodity but a powerful component of mindfulness. Allocating periods of digital silence allows the mind to reset, creating space for introspection and mental clarity. This doesn't mean disconnecting entirely; it's about consciously choosing moments of quiet and reflection amidst connectivity. Silence, then, becomes a form of self-care, nourishing the mind much like water hydrates the body.

As we carve out these silent sanctuaries, we must also seek to balance the influx of information. The more information we consume, the harder it becomes to digest. Curating digital content thoughtfully allows us to focus on information that enriches rather than exhaust us. Embracing the art of saying "no" to unnecessary digital clutter can be liberating. We can practice this by unsubscribing from unneeded communications and unfollowing sources that don't align with our mindfulness goals.

Our constant connection offers both challenges and opportunities. While it can be overwhelming, it's also a gateway to enhanced self-awareness and connection with others. Through mindful engagement, technology can open avenues to explore new philosophies and insights, helping us grow. The key is maintaining an attitude of curiosity and openness while recognizing when digital interactions detract from our wellbeing.

Social media often represents the forefront of continuous connectivity, and it's imperative to approach these platforms with caution. Understanding the impact of our screen time on mental health is crucial. One strategy is to set intentions before engaging with social media—decide what you aim to gain before logging in. Be it connection, inspiration, or just a momentary distraction, knowing your purpose can help prevent the traps of endless scrolling.

Furthermore, utilizing settings to limit screen time or employ apps specifically designed to enhance productivity can also be beneficial. These tools act as digital allies, helping keep your moments connected to purpose, whether it's during work hours or personal downtime. This symmetry between technology and intentionality fosters a harmonious digital presence.

For some, the concept of continuous connection feels like a tether, yet it doesn't have to be restrictive. Instead, preparing for it can be an empowering journey towards mastering digital engagement without losing self-awareness. As you learn to harmonize with technology, notice how it can actually enhance your practice of mindfulness itself— reminding you to breathe amidst chaos or focus amidst distractions.

Prepare not by perceiving technology as the enemy, but as a component of the modern landscape that, with mindful navigation, can enrich your life. Embrace it with a wise mind and open heart, and you'll find continuous connection can be less about being always available and more about being continually present wherever you choose to be.

Ultimately, preparing for continuous connection is about crafting a digital habitat that is consciously connected. Engage in practices that foster longer periods of focus and peace, ensuring your digital life supports a mindful existence. In doing so, you're not just preparing for a future that's digitally connected—you're crafting one that is mindfully lived.

Conclusion

As we've journeyed through this exploration of digital mindfulness, it's clear that the intersection of technology and mindfulness offers a unique opportunity to harmonize our lives. We've seen how the relentless noise of digital devices can drown out the quiet spaces that foster inner peace. Yet, we've also discovered pathways to reclaim those spaces, even within our digital interactions. The essence of this book has been to illustrate how technology, when approached with mindfulness, doesn't have to be a barrier to tranquility, but rather a bridge.

The digital world is vast and often overwhelming, yet through mindful practice, it becomes a landscape of potential calm rather than chaos. Embracing the roots of mindfulness, we can nurture a presence that persists even as screens flicker and notifications ping. By intentionally choosing how we engage online, such as through conscious social media practices or cultivating awareness in our digital communications, we shape a digital existence that aligns with our values.

One of our greatest challenges is to manage digital stress and the multifaceted interactions that come with it. Learning to set boundaries, creating digital detox periods, and adopting digital minimalism are crucial to maintaining balance. The art of mindful communication, alongside the role of active listening, redefines how we interact, ensuring that our connections remain meaningful and empathetic.

Technology has also provided us with tools for mindfulness, which, when used wisely, can enhance rather than detract from our life satisfaction. These tools, whether apps or gadgets, can remind us to pause, breathe, and refocus. However, the key lies not in the tool itself but in our commitment to using it mindfully. Posture your digital life so that it's an extension of your mindful practices, not the other way around.

In workplaces everywhere, setting boundaries between work and digital rest becomes ever more crucial in preventing burnout. The strategies we've discussed emphasize techniques for achieving true downtime, thereby bolstering both productivity and overall well-being. Similarly, when faced with endless streams of media and information, adopting a practice of critical evaluation enables us to navigate this digital deluge with clarity and confidence.

Moreover, integrating mindfulness with the burgeoning advancements in AI offers new dynamics to explore. As AI continues to shape our attention economy, understanding its impact becomes imperative. We are encouraged to integrate AI tools mindfully, ensuring they amplify rather than diminish our capacity for attention and presence.

Intriguingly, our relationships have also been redefined in this digital era, with opportunities for nurturing connections that transcend physical spaces. Mindful practices guide us in avoiding pitfalls of miscommunication and fostering deeper connection through technology. We extend these practices into family life, crafting a balanced home environment and fostering healthy habits for media consumption among children.

The creative realm hasn't been ignored, as mindful consumption of content invites a deeper appreciation and inspiration. Moreover, new technologies like virtual reality present unique opportunities for meditation and inner peace, paving the way for future mindfulness practices.

For those in leadership positions, this mindful journey holds particular resonance. As digital leaders, the emphasis on developing conscious qualities and leading with presence stands out, ensuring that technology doesn't overshadow but enhances human connection.

As we look forward, the future of digital mindfulness is one of continual adaptation and reflection. Emerging trends will provide new opportunities to engage and redefine our relationships with technology, keeping in mind the importance of privacy, security, and the environmental impact of our digital choices.

Ultimately, the core of this journey lies in our ability to find balance, to stand firm amidst the rapid transformations of the digital landscape while nurturing a tranquil heart. May the principles outlined become a beacon, guiding you towards a life where technology and mindfulness coexist harmoniously, enriching your existence in profound and enduring ways.

Appendix A: Appendix

In this Appendix, we gather a thoughtfully curated collection of resources for those seeking to deepen their understanding and practice of digital mindfulness. Moving beyond the chapters, these resources include books, articles, and websites that delve into the harmony between technology and mindful living. Whether you're interested in exploring foundational theories or looking for practical applications to integrate into your daily routines, this compilation aims to inspire and guide further learning. By engaging with these materials, you'll uncover new perspectives and tools to cultivate a mindful digital presence and embrace a balanced, technology-enhanced lifestyle. Dive in, explore, and let your journey of mindful technology use flourish.

Resources for Further Reading

Exploring the realm of digital mindfulness is a journey that doesn't end with the final page of this book. It's a continuous process of learning, adapting, and integrating new insights into your digital existence. To ensure you have ample pathways for further exploration, here are some resources that align with the principles discussed in the previous chapters.

Books can serve as foundational guides, offering a deeper understanding of the intertwined nature of technology and mindfulness. A notable mention would be 'Digital Minimalism' by Cal Newport, which delves into the philosophy of stripping back digital clutter to create a more intentional tech experience. Another imperative read is 'The Art of Mindful Communication' by Thich Nhat Hanh, which is particularly beneficial for those who wish to enhance their communication skills in an increasingly online world.

For those who prefer auditory learning, podcasts can be a brilliant resource. The podcast 'The Digital Mindfulness Podcast' explores myriad aspects of maintaining mindfulness while using technology. It's a resource that's regularly updated, ensuring the content is fresh and relevant, with guest experts bringing varied perspectives. Episodes can be streamed during a mindful walk or while unwinding after a long day.

Academic journals provide insights into the scientific and psychological underpinnings of mindfulness practices in the digital era. Journals such as the 'Journal of Technology in Behavioral Science' often publish articles on the impact of technology on mental health and strategies for fostering digital wellness. Accessing these articles might require institutional access, but they're invaluable for those interested in research-backed information.

Online platforms and blogs focused on mindfulness and digital wellness often provide both practical tips and community support. Websites like 'Mindful.org' host a variety of articles, meditations, and webinars that cater to those seeking balance in their connected lives. Joining their community forums can also provide a space to share experiences and gain insights from others on a similar journey.

If you're inclined towards structured learning, online courses can be a fantastic way to delve deeper into the topics discussed in this book. Platforms like Coursera and Udemy offer courses related to digital minimalism, mindfulness practices, and even how to manage digital stress. These courses often come with flexible time commitments, allowing you to progress at your own pace.

Documentaries can offer a visual understanding of the impact of technology on our everyday lives and our environment. Films such as 'The Social Dilemma' examine the influence of social media and digital platforms, with a keen eye on how these technologies affect mental well-being and social interactions. Watching such documentaries in a mindful setting can further enhance your understanding of digital mindfulness.

For those interested in interactive and introspective exploration, apps designed for mindfulness can be highly beneficial. Applications like 'Headspace' and 'Calm' offer guided meditations and exercises that focus on being present amidst the backdrop of a tech-centric world. These apps can be conveniently accessed on mobile devices, allowing you to integrate mindfulness practices into your daily routine seamlessly.

Attending workshops or retreats can provide an immersive experience, offering a chance to disconnect from digital stimuli and reconnect with the self. Such events often focus on practical strategies for achieving digital balance, supported by community and expert leaders. They create opportunities for deep reflection and the cultivation of new habits.

Engaging with community groups or forums, whether online or offline, can provide support and motivation. Platforms like Meetup have groups that host discussions or activities centered around mindfulness in tech use. Such interactions not only broaden your understanding but also reinforce your commitment to leading a mindful digital life.

Finally, staying informed about emerging trends in technology and mindfulness can be accomplished by following thought leaders and experts on social media platforms like Twitter and LinkedIn. They often share articles, insights, and tips that can keep you ahead in terms of practices and strategies for digital mindfulness.

Your path to digital mindfulness is your own to carve. The resources listed above are starting points, gateways to a world of information that can inspire and guide your journey. As you continue to explore and implement strategies from this book, these resources will support your evolution toward leading a more harmonious digital life.

www.ingramcontent.com/pod-product-compliance
Lightning Source LLC
LaVergne TN
LVHW051345050326
832903LV00031B/3756